AFTER THE PITCH

Copyright © 2021 by Adrian T. Marable

All rights reserved. No part of this book may be reproduced in any manner whatsoever without written permission except in the case of brief quotations embodied in critical articles and reviews.

First Printing, 2021

AFTER THE PITCH

How to Think Like an Investor and Secure the Startup Funding You Deserve

ADRIAN T. MARABLE

Beloda Publishing

Beloda Publishing

CONTENTS

Resources	vii
Preface	1
Chapter One: The Pitch	5
Chapter Two: Preparation	20
Chapter Three: Rules of Engagement	39
Chapter Four: Lessons From Investors	58
Chapter Five : Choosing the Right Investor	76
Chapter Six: Diligence	88
Chapter Seven: Beyond Due Diligence	106
Chapter Eight: Team/Founders	117
Chapter Nine: Commercial	141
Chapter Ten: Market	160
Chapter Eleven: Legal	178
Chapter Twelve: Financials	187
Chapter Thirteen: Product or Service Specific	212
Chapter Fourteen: Industry-Specific	225

Pitch Dictionary 237

About The Author 247

RESOURCES

MASTER OPERATIONAL ENTREPRENEURSHIP
Go to AdrianMarable.com/resources to get bonus materials, access additional resources, join our private community, and more.

DEDICATION

To my wife, Ebony, for being my support through late nights and early mornings. I know I can always look for you to make me a better man for God sent me you for this very purpose.

For my daughter, Payton, who attended more business meetings (before the age 5) than any other child that I know. You are my light in the most cloudy days. I believe you can do the impossible.

To my mom for supporting my successes and education when others around me were nothing but roadblocks.

To my dad who always taught me that hard work, consistency and building great relationships are the best ways to survive in this world.

To my investment partners and friends, Brandon and Willayna. Without you, I would have never written this book.

Preface

For many years, I worked with professionals to help them develop their careers. I've studied high performing executives and entrepreneurs to figure out what makes them tick and what makes them successful. Using what I've learned helped not only my career, but many others excel in their career path. As I continue my journey, I keep finding many people who want to know how I did it, what I've learned, and how can they follow a similar path. My dream is to start a private equity firm as a way of growing businesses, providing inclusion and empowering cultures. I am still on track to obtain my dream and as a new angel investor, I have an amazing look at the world of business and funding.

On this journey, I studied, journaled, and read everything possible to make sure I can take on this new role. I've had the opportunity to talk with hundreds of entrepreneurs and watch them from pitch to growth (sometimes to failure). I've listened to famous angel investors and VCs such as Mark Cuban, Tony Clark, and Sequoia Capital as they give their insights into the world of startup funding. From my studies and experiences, I compiled what I've learned and done to give you a perspective of the due diligence process to help both investors and startup founders.

Since I can remember, helping people made me the happiest. Seeing the look of appreciation on their faces, regardless of what act of kindness I did, felt good to me. People do not have to show appreciation to me. I enjoy helping people by providing them with convenience or ease they would not otherwise receive. My love for helping people is why I wrote this book.

Due diligence is the most important part of fundraising. Since investors can see hundreds or even thousands of founders each year and only a few receive investment, it's important to make a good impression. Ninety percent of the funding process for an investor is due-diligence. My fellow investors and I work on, start and end with due diligence. To be honest, rarely is due diligence spoken about unless you're deep into the startup world. You seldom hear about it on TV or podcasts. When you Google due diligence, often you find long boring college lectures with a special guest speaker who has been in corporate finance for decades. Let's face it, just hearing the words "due diligence" doesn't sound glamorous or sexy. If you've been through it, you know it's far from a stimulating activity. The exciting part is the pitch. The pitch is why shows such as *Shark Tank* and *Elevator Pitch* are so successful. Because of these shows, some details do not seem to matter as much, but they do! As a founder, know as much about your business as possible. As an investor, know exactly what's important for you to understand in the business you're interested in.

This book covers the areas due diligence can entail. It will help you prepare, but not go into the nitty gritty financial details to spare you the financial work you already know or you will probably hire someone to look over for you. This book lists over 200 questions an investor can ask a founder and explains the importance of each of those questions. At times, questions may seem stupid or redundant, but there's usually a reason why an investor asks a particular question. Either it's because of the importance to them as an investor, or it's because of a concern they have. Overall, this is the book I wish I had years before entering the startup world.

I have my own experiences pitching as a startup founder and being pitched as an angel investor. My first tech startup received three offers for funding before I fully developed the technology. The pitch I had rehearsed hundreds of times. I had it down, and it sounded like a natural conversation. Still, I lost pitch competitions and had investors repeatedly tell me they were not interested or did not like my idea. It's part of the world of angel and VC investing. Not everything is cut and dry, not everyone will like your idea (at least not initially) which is another reason why I wrote this book.

There are investors right now still kicking themselves for not investing in Apple, Uber, or Airbnb among many other disruptors, but rest assure if you realize pitching is a numbers game, you will eventually receive a bite or two. Where it goes completely wrong for both the investor and founder happens after the pitch.

Through my own pitches as a founder, listening to pitches as a spectator and investor, and asking questions as an investor, I have amassed this book. They were the questions I wanted to know as a founder and more importantly as a new investor working with seasoned venture capital and angel organizations. I've also sprinkled in some tips and examples from the perspective of other investors through interviews I've had with them.

To make the most out of this book, let me explain the format. I broke this book down into two parts.

Part one of the book is about "the process" of what happens after your pitch. No process or system is the same, but I lay out the foundation based on how I and other investors complete their due diligence. Though I will address the founder more often in this section, it's important for investors to determine their own due diligence process.

Part two is the question-and-answer section. Here I address the perspectives of the investor and why a founder should understand. The questions are not random. They all have a purpose or are a part of the process. A founder doesn't always see this, but it will give them an advantage over other startups.

In the back of the book, I placed a pitch dictionary. If you're new and unsure of a term in this book, reference there to get a brief explanation. I hope to hear how this book helps you on your journey to obtaining the funding you need or giving money to a growing startup. Enjoy.

Chapter One: The Pitch

My First Pitch

Have you pitched your business yet? If you haven't and you are looking for funding, you will likely have some of the same feelings I felt during my first pitch. The feeling of anxiety as you wait for your name to be called or as you walk into the pitch meeting/room. You're finally in front of an investor or group of investors and if it's your first time, it becomes the most terrifying moment in your business life! You think, anything could go wrong in your pitch during a moment which seems to slow down just long enough to load your mind with negative thoughts. Despite rehearsing for hours and hours at a time, you feel if you blow it, you have forever proved your business is a failure. If you succeed, you acquire the much needed funding you wanted to give your startup some breathing room for a few months at the least.

Finally, you're right in front of the successful investors. As your body becomes stiff, you're sweating for no reason and your body is shaking to a point it feels like an earthquake. Luckily, it's only noticeable to you and not the investors sitting directly in front of you. You take a deep breath and you belt out your lines like you've rehearsed hundreds of times in front of your mirror, your friends, and your board of advisors. After a few minutes, you're done. You landed the pitch, word for word just like you practiced.

My wife and I compare this feeling to having a baby. You are in your own bubble developing this "thing". Months go by and you finally have something you produced. Something you can present to the world. But what if your baby is ugly and no one likes it? What if all the love and care you put into producing this baby ends in it not being accepted by the people who you want most to love it? Now that you've presented your baby to the world, what comes next?

I've pitched my businesses to investors, and I've been fairly successful in receiving funding offers. My first tech startup secured three offers for funding before the developers finished building the technology. My pitch? I rehearsed it hundreds of times. I could even say I mastered it to the point it sounded like a natural conversation. What I did not prepare for consisted of what happened after the pitch and after being offered funding. Why would I have been prepared? As a founder, my job consisted of pitching my business. That's it! An idea I vetted out for about a year. With no revenue, the product remained unfinished, and I still didn't know how to truly execute my launch.

The first time I pitched my business, the nerves shot through my body like arrows. I entered a pitch contest for an incubator program I gained accepted into. Even though I felt prepared to present my pitch, I became more terrified of the question and answer session at the end of the pitch. All the startup founders were given two minutes to pitch their ideas or currently running startups. Two minutes to explain every facet of their business (well at least their most important parts) with no slides and no demo of how it worked. For a new founder, it seemed like an impossible feat. I wrote the pitch with the help of my board of advisors. I wrote, we tweaked, and I wrote some more until we thought we developed an impactful pitch. I became comfortable with my pitch once I wrote it. Two years prior, I joined Toastmasters because according to my wife, it looked like I could easily pass out when I spoke in front of people. To this day, I thank Toastmasters for how much they helped me become a better speaker. The day of the pitch, I would have likely passed out just off the principle there were over 100 people in the room staring down at me in an auditorium.

Watching the other pitches didn't make me feel any better. All my fellow incubator members were doing amazing at explaining their startup. Some were pitching better than I ever heard them pitch before. When they finally announced my number, I stood up there, looked up at my +100 person audience, grabbed the microphone off of the stand (something no one else did in the competition so far) and belted out my pitch. My startup idea was a online group study platform that helped people who wanted to form exam prep study groups virtually. The format of the programs and the features of the technology may have made it a revolutionary product. I just needed to know if the judges felt the same way.

Starting with a brief story of feeling lousy in my career, I asked the audience if they've ever felt lost the way I did in the story of my life. Per Toastmasters, starting with a story and question is a great way to engage the audience. I received the head nods and a couple of people mouthing the words "yes!" In a brief milli-second I thought to myself, "Just like I imagined it would happen, I have them hooked!" I kept going and at one minute and 55 seconds, I completed my pitch! It was over! Well, not really.

After the applause, I think I only heard the eerie silence permeating the room (yes, I heard the silence). As the judges passed their microphone around, I received my first question and comment. The comment came first..."I see the benefits of your product but I personally don't like group studying!" The takeout punch! Imagine being hit in the kidney by Mike Tyson but unable to physically express the pain. Internally, I doubled over and screamed in agony with no chance of getting back up. At the time, no one ever told me they didn't like my startup idea. I could barely think. Internally I stumbled back to my feet in what felt like a last ditch ever to recover and save face. Besides, whoever wants to be knocked out with the first punch? Plus, I'm a fighter. Not literally but mentally. I answered all the questions in the fog of thoughts circulating the words"... personally I don't like group studying!" There were several questions I completely knew the answers to while there were others I knew but over explained or vaguely answered. I knew I could have answered most of the questions better AFTER I sat back down at my seat.

I did not bomb it, but I didn't do spectacular either. Needless to say, I didn't win the pitch contest, but within a week, I secured two investors. One from the pitch contest and another who I delivered the same pitch to a couple of days later. What happened after the pitch became the worse part of the contest for me. I didn't do my best in the Q&A portion. Those who won the competition, obviously provided clear and concise answers to the judges' questions which caused them to win. Some of the winners received no more funding after the pitch competition while I managed to secure the funding I needed to move my idea forward. I attribute this to my level of work ethic and the preparation I put forth during the incubator to vet out my idea. Still, the preparation I needed to interact with any investor after they were interested in writing my startup a check did not exist. Goes to show you even when you're knocked out, you can still get up and be a winner. Even if it's the next fight.

Even thought I acquired funding, I kicked myself repeatedly for weeks over the competition which in turn motivated me. I ended up researching questions I may be asked in the future. I wanted to be prepared and if I stumbled on another question, I could at least pick myself up on the next one. After reading different books, I found literature on how to pitch but nothing to prepare me for all the questions I would receive after. Nothing comforted my feelings and concerns of unpreparedness. Most of the due diligence books and materials were all about mergers and acquisitions (M&A). The private equity activities I aspire to achieve one day. M&A due diligence is a lot more thorough as it should be but encompasses some of the same activities, requests and principles. Usually the more money involved, the more vetting the investor must complete. Think of the difference, startups are usually less established and growth, sales, and even operations are not consistent or nonexistent. Established companies on the other hand have standard reporting of income statements, balance sheets, tax filings, and profit/loss statements. This helps make the request for records clear for established organizations but not so much for startups. Thus, this book is born.

    Not always done in the infamous *Shark Tank* format, you may not pitch standing in front of a panel of investors to receive money. Like me, you could be standing in the middle of a group of people with only a few being investors. Many times, pitching is not so formal unless you're pitching to a syndicate of investors or for a television show. Sometimes you're pitching in unconventional places. It could be at a restaurant, golf course, coffee shop, or even while taking a walk down the street. This means, no slides, no videos, just pure conversation with your potential investor. My first pitch competition came in handy in this regard. If you're comfortable pitching and your idea is great, you have a better chance at acquiring at the least a second meeting with a potential investor. It's a numbers game. Some people will like your idea while others will not. There are tons of people who did not invest in Facebook, Twitter or Uber. They still managed to expand to large companies.

    Pitching is done and you have potential investors on the hook. Now what? The event historically destroying the funding rounds of founders. No matter how outstanding or terrible you present your pitch, responding to the investors' specific asks is important. It is the first line of defense in determining if you procure funding or not. These asks start directly after your pitch, into due diligence if the investor decides to fund you, and even further into the life of you and your investor's relationship together. Due diligence can last days, months, and in few cases I am familiar with, up to almost a year. Do not worry, investors understand the criticality of funding and it normally takes 30 to 60 days to thrust through due diligence for a new startup. Once again, it depends on the size of the investment and the investor's preferences. Studies express most investors who spend more time on completing due diligence receive higher returns. Every investor has their own process to verify if your business is really worth them injecting capital before the check is deposited into your business account. Your due diligence process will also vary according to the type of business being evaluated and the stage of growth your business is in.

For those experienced in pitching, the most solid start to developing your business pitch is by putting together a detailed business plan. This plan gives you a structure of what investors want to know about your business during due diligence.

If your startup is already generating revenue, investors like to first hear about the traction you've gained and then into your business model and financials. Traction is what strikes an investors attention. Be careful in misstating or misrepresenting your traction or any other data you have around your business. Doing so could ruin your chances of funding as well. You must be credible and extremely transparent with your data gathering and presentation. If your startup is not already generating revenue, the data around market opportunity is key. Among the data, investors invest in the founder(s) and the team. Founders must be able to inspire investors, their team, customers, media and fellow innovators. Communicating who you are and your brand as a founder is what makes this possible. Communication is key. Steve Jobs is one of the most visionary minds of all but more importantly, his passion and communication skills created the "*Apple Culture.*" Even if you are not pitching your business, it's usually the startup founders who must present a clear message and sale their product or service to potential customers.

Becoming an Investor

Today, I not only have several businesses, but I also invest in startup companies. I've watched people over the years pitch their businesses and have analyzed the similarities of the businesses who lose the deal after the pitch. This is usually where it happens. I've sat in on other investors' meetings and due diligence processes as well as gone through my own. I've taken away many ideas from investors I've used for my own business but have also been disturbed by the practices of some of my other fellow investors. With superb and immoral practices comes lessons learned.

Investing is different than most other careers I've come across. It takes a lot of the same skills such as analysis, strategy, operational and technical knowledge, but at the end of the day everything is speculative. Investors invest because of their own beliefs. They don't always go by facts and figures. Investor can choose to invest or not invest based on someone's sex, race, age, or background. It's common for investors to invest in people who look like them and have a similar background as they do. That's without even considering if their idea is exceptional or not. This explains the separation of the races and genders who receive more or less funding. Luckily there are both people and organizations who are creating awareness around this inequity. Also, more investors are investing in a wider range of companies and finding ways to take an unbiased look when considering capital injection. I believe though I invest in a founder or set of co-founders, I invest in who they are, how their values correlate with mine, and not what they look like.

My first investor's meeting I would describe as very informal. I wouldn't even consider myself an investor at this time though the ask from me would result in providing significant seed funding for an inexperienced startup company near the Charlotte, North Carolina Area. It took place in one late November when I received a tip from a close friend and former business partner about a husband/wife team who wanted to expand their successful food truck business by opening up a brick and mortar restaurant. Beyond watching *Shark Tank* and *The Profit*, what investing entailed rose beyond my knowledge. What I did know is about people. I spent the first part of my career in heavy sales jobs and have been fortunate enough to interact with every class of person imaginable. When I mean class, I mean every age, race, sex, education level, social status, etc. Besides being able to pick the best pitches on *Shark Tank* 98% of the time, I couldn't spot a good business if it slapped me in the face. I've always been business oriented since my mom taught me how to count money as a little boy. My dad taught me all about relationships and how first impressions mean so much. Building on those two skills made me very successful up until then but it didn't teach me about forecasting business success based on a founder, their team, or the company's business model. It didn't teach me about tell-tell signs of a poor investment. To tell you why I didn't invest would be better accomplished by telling you the story of how the day went.

 I pulled up to an old strip mall which looked like a scene out of the 80s. Imagine, an old shopping center in an area located about 3 miles off of an interstate which once seemed to be a small bustling town. Most of the big brand fast food joints and gas stations already occupied the spaces within a half mile of the interstate and I am sure their real estate costs were at a premium. What I knew about restaurants and still believe about the restaurant industry is the success of a restaurant is all about location, location, location! The same friend who tipped me off on this potential investment came with me and also expressed his interest in investing. He owned a business in the food services industry and it made me more comfortable with him being there with me. Besides location, I knew nothing about the restaurant industry. As an investor, I now know something which would have given me back over two hours of my life. How founders represent themselves (or show up) when you first meet them is usually how they'll show up after you invest in their company and start working with them. Like my dad taught me, first impressions are everything. The first issue with this guy? He showed up late. His wife did not attend because she still ran food truck side of their business. After all, she's the head chef. He's the sales and brand guy of the business. It's only right he be the person to pitch I guess. Still, he showed up late. Not a few minutes late, extremely late. Even after we finally met him, he never apologized for taking up our time.

We walked through the current restaurant setup. It still showed signs of major renovations needed and the landlord provided the owners a rent-free period to renovate before their lease payments started. The co-owner nevertheless wanted us to see "his vision" for the location. We started from the back of the building, slowly moving our way to the front of the restaurant. His vision seemed grand yet unrealistic to me. He mostly portrayed transparency when speaking about his business except when it came to the costs he was about to incur. Luckily my friend's expertise spotted his discrepancies in the numbers. You have to know your numbers! In some other cases he went back on some of the information he presented to us previously. He told us about the ups and the downs of the location and how everything worked down to the pieces of equipment and safety issues needing to be fixed. He showed to be quite a sales guy and made sure no stone remained unturned when it came to him selling us "his vision". He even offered to put our names on the wall and provide us free meals anytime we stopped by the restaurant. At every other opportunity, he made sure to complement our intelligence and level of business savvy. I give the guy an "A+" for effort.

After over two and a half hours of hearing about "his vision" and him answering questions, we walked outside. What I remember the most about the location is as soon as I walked out the front door, there were almost a dozen restaurants within eye shot of me. Half were small chains and the other half consisted of mom and pop shops. Another red flag I now recognize quickly were the words, "Rent is low" and "This used to be a booming area." Just to humor myself, I asked the owner who did he consider his competition and without any pause he said, "NOBODY! I have no competition in this area." I'll speak more on why "NOBODY" is the worst answer he or any founder could provide and why he thought it to be the correct answer later in this book.

I give the meeting a three out of ten if I could rate all the investor meetings I've participated in so far. They served a great product. People loved the product as well. Their current business model with the food truck created sustainability but they were looking to translate it into an untested market for them. Food trucks are different than brick and mortar stores which means there must be a different business model (even if it's a slight change). Most of their business consisted of being in the heart of Charlotte, not on the outskirts. The owner's grandiose vision for this small place presented cost concerns for an (at the time) unfunded businesses just starting out. Per my friend who accompanied me and introduced us, his equipment costs were going to be astronomical and he kept ranting about buying brand new toilets so the one toilet in the men's room matched the one in the women's room. No one should even notice there's a difference or allow that to be why they rate a company. Well maybe if it is was a toilet company! I personally prefer the companies I work with be lean in the way they operate. I would have preferred the owner say they're buying something like a toilet at a discounted rate at a Salvation Army or Goodwill warehouse. The biggest concern for me included the co-owner's lack of general business sense and the inability to agree with his wife on operations which he openly admitted to. A complimentary co-founder relationship is a must, especially if it's a husband/wife team. I should know since my wife and I co-found a company together. After providing my list of constructive criticism to him and ways I would personally be able to help him, I never heard from him again. The brick and mortar ended up going out of business before it even started. He failed to obtain enough funding and those who invested lost their money. The food truck is still running quite successfully.

Since then I've become much wiser as an investor. I've become a student of investing and what happens at different stages and rounds of startup investing. This book is to help you understand from both the perspective of the founder and the investor. Pitching is great, but it only places your foot in the door. If an investor invests in your business only from your pitch, I would hope it's only from a person who knows you. Experienced Investors want two things...the highest return possible and the lowest risk possible. Most importantly for me is high return. To determine this, due diligence is a priority for me. If you can answer these three questions upfront with 100% certainty in a way in which it satisfies the investor, you are off to a great start. **These are the basics:**

1. How much money do you want?
2. How much work you want me to do for the money?
3. When and how will I receive my money back?

When it comes to angel investors, it doesn't really matter how much money you want, but more of how much they are willing to give you. How much you want only determines your valuation for them. Therefore most investor do not go straight into these three questions and more broadly they want to know the answer to these five questions.

1. What problem are you trying to solve?
2. How is your solution/approach unique?
3. How is it sustainable?
4. Is this problem ready to be solved?
5. When/How will you make money?

If you're interested in receiving venture capital, if it doesn't make dollars, it doesn't make sense. Many venture capitalists and private equity firms obtain their reputation from providing a return to their pool of investors who invest in their funds. Yes, they invest in founders, they invest in ideas, but once again, they invest for the perceived value/returns they look to receive. No investor has ever said, "I'm going to invest in this to lose money."

Okay, you can stop reading now, you have everything you need to know to acquire all the seed investment you want! If it were only so simple.

A lot of effort goes into investing and to make the big bucks, you must put the time and effort into your own business and its processes to make the right investor decision and the right investment decision. After listening to hundreds of pitches and going through numerous due diligence processes, it's important you know what your own processes/systems are. What are you willing and unwilling to provide the investor? What type of investor is best for your company? Do they understand your business and your vision as a founder? Are they focused on long-term growth of your startup? Who does the work of being the point(s) of contact during the investor's process? There's a lot of questions to ask yourself and there's a lot of tasks to execute. It's this book and the experiences inside of it which will prepare you for those tasks.

Getting Started with this Book

So, who is this book for? I wrote this book with two types of people in mind. First, the startup founder and his or her team looking for startup capital. Obtaining funding is hard enough without the stresses of going through the due diligence process of acquiring funding. It could be as painful as going through the process of receiving a business loan or having several of your teeth pulled with little medication. Once you have your structure created however, you can almost put your process on autopilot. Not only will your team be ready to go through due diligence, you and also your clients (if you are already generating revenue) will be prepared. Yes, some of your key customers/clients can likely be included in the due diligence process with you and they need to be just a prepared as your company will be.

Secondly, the book is written for the startup investor. Whether you be unseasoned to investing, just started a syndicate of angels, or you're looking to revise your due diligence process, this book is also a guide to thinking differently about your business. Many people do not understand investing though they have a strong interest to invest in startups. It's trendy, it's fun, and it can bring great returns for those with disposable income. The problem I see, is a novice investor will invest in a startup based solely on the pitch. Months later, they've received no return, no update on how the startup is doing, the startup has folded, and essentially the investor's money is gone. I also see people invest illegitimately into a startup. They're not qualified investors and they do not invest in accordance to the government's guidelines. More often than not, they too lose their money. Money they could not afford to lose. This comes from lack of both investor and founder knowledge. For the experienced investor, some of this may be elementary, however I expect you will learn something from reading this book as well.

Now you understand who I am and why this book, it's only right to tell you how to use this book properly. I recommend you do three activities to successfully utilize this book. Think of it as a toolkit for your funding life. Keep it in your bag, on your desk, or wherever you prefer to read. You should read the remainder of this book in three different ways.

1. **Skim it.** If you just read this book and put it down, you're going to miss some parts. You will not be as prepared to use the information or answer the questions in this book without skimming it first. Readers tend to become stuck in the weeds during the first read through which leads them to not finishing the book and seeing vital parts they'll need during their own due diligence process. Once you have reviewed the entire book , turn on your thinking cap and take the next step of reading it in its entirety.
2. **Read it in its entirety.** Now you have an idea of all the sections and the questions entailed, think about your business. In the question and answer section, see if you can answer every question about your business. Even though this book covers many of the possible processes and information you would need to provide investors and their team, every investor will have a different process.
3. **Reference it**. Because there are a vast number of questions related to your business, it's only appropriate to revisit these questions. As your business evolves, your answers will change as well as become clearer. The due diligence process will also change as you go through different rounds of funding and/or start working with different types of investors. Founders use the question section as a guide on not only how to build their business plans but how to work better with their investment partners.

Most of the questions come with explanations on why an investor would ask a question. Some also include stories, anecdotes, and examples on how you can respond as a founder. Many times, questions are asked because of the lack of knowledge or a concern the investor has in your business model. Investors use the question section to determine what to ask startup founders before providing them with funding. It's always smart to go back and reference the questions even after you feel like you're prepared for due diligence or have already gone through it several times. For an investor, going back to reference some of these questions will spark new questions in areas you may be concerned about.

Chapter Two: Preparation

Business Maturity

What happens after the pitch? The brief answer is the investor decides whether to provide funding. If they want to, you go through the due diligence process. Due Diligence is a period where the investor validates if your business is investable. During this time, the founder also determines if the investor is worth working with. If the investor gives you money for your business, they will likely in exchange ask for a percentage of ownership in your company called equity. The equity percentage also determines the percentage of return the investor will receive from the money they invest. This provides more incentive for new investors to help the startup grow.

Investors treat your business based on two factors; the stage of investment you are in and the type of business you are running. The funding stage and type of investor in most cases goes hand-in-hand. The "pre-revenue stage" is the earliest stage of funding. Pre-revenue companies are those companies who have not officially launched their product or service but have received a lot of interest and/ or solved a unique problem. Within the pre-revenue stage, the first unofficial rounds of funding start with you and your co-founder's injection of capital.

Friends, Family, and Fools (FFF)

Beyond your own investment, you may pitch your business to your friends and family (often called FFF meaning Friends, Family, and Fools). These people typically invest in you and what sounds like a superb idea. They may ask for a business plan, but they will often base their investment off their disposable income, how much they like you, and what you pitch them. Rarely do they require a lengthy due diligence process or you to answer a list of investor questions. You're possibly offering them incentives to complete the injection of seed capital into your business like equity, free services, a free product with upgrades, etc.

The first investors leverage their value early and can take advantage of their position as the only one or one of few people who have invested. With no great way to value the business properly, smart founders offer single digit equity percentages for capital in the beginning. It's not uncommon for a startup to only provide 2%-5% ownership in an FFF round.

Let me repeat this to you as a founder because it's important. Investors complete the due diligence process at this stage in short order. Unless your FFF round consists of someone business and/or technical savvy, the founder can find funding with the least effort. Also, not all investments are excellent investments. If due diligence creates too much unnecessary work, you may not want that investor to commit to your business because they'll continue to put you through the ringer. This segment of funders will mainly invest purely off trust, love and the capital they have to give you. Those who are savvy will want a demo of the product or service and probably sit down with you to "go over the numbers." It is advised you treat even your FFF who are interested in your business with the same patience and respect as you would any other investor. Too often founders skip over the FFF round since they think they do not know wealthy people. Sometimes it takes a little networking to find friends or family capable of investing in your startup. I encourage you to take some time to determine who those people are. This will improve your chances of ramping up your first funding round quickly. Friends, family, and fools should be able to inject $3,000 or more into your business. If you're at a higher valuation, you may require a minimum investment amount from each investor.

When friends and family are not an option, most founders start pitching their pre-revenue business to angel investors (Angels). Angels are those who invest their own money into a startup. Traditionally, angels like to target startups who have just come out of the friends and family round and have not gained an immense amount of traction. Since they're only investing their money, you'll find the average investor in this category willing to inject between $25,000 and $100,000 into your business.

Angels

Looking for angel investors is easy. Receiving the first investment is the most difficult. Finding the "right" investor and investment is an even different monster. You will find them online, at pitch competitions, open calls to pitch and business conferences. Companies such as AngelList, Kickstarter, Indiegogo, and the Angel Capital Association are great resources to start your search. Remember, the key role of a startup founder looking for funding is to network. Through networking, you will significantly increase your reach through the theory of six degrees of separation. You could be two people away from meeting a millionaire or billionaire looking to invest in a company like yours. Do not neglect finding investors through the people you already work with like your fellow entrepreneurs, lawyers, accountants, and bankers. These people are around other people in the business world who have money. Don't limit yourself to local investors. There are investors all over the world who may invest in your company, and with today's technology, it doesn't always require you to travel all around the world. Limiting yourself closes the window of opportunity quickly. Venture out if you truly desire to have your company funded.

For an angel investor, the jackpot is finding a startup you feel can be an industry disrupter. Like I said, Angels are individuals who put in their own money to invest into a startup company. Larger returns are received if the startup they invest in has found a gap in an industry or found a major way to innovate within the industry. Think about Amazon who disrupted bookstores, Uber who disrupted taxi services, or even Netflix who disrupted movie stores such as Blockbuster.

It may take investors time to understand the vision of your product or service when your startup is in the ideation stage. Good investors have a knack for seeing the vision when there's no tangible evidence of success. The type of funding a founder should be looking for at this point is called seed capital or seed investment. To reduce the risk for an angel investor, they may choose to provide funding as a convertible note versus an equity stake. This means your investor is giving you a loan but optionally can decide to turn the loan into an equity ownership into your business based on how successful your business becomes during a predetermined period of time. This is great for the founder who does not want to give up equity immediately and will have an opportunity to payback the investor which makes the investor feel comfortable about taking the investment risk.

Rounds of Investing

Your first and second official rounds (called series A and B respectively) of investment happen at an early stage of the startup where you now have a product and may gain some traction or acquired your first handful of customers. At the least you have your idea laid out and need larger capital injections to bring the product or service to market. This is where angels may still hang around, but angel syndicates, venture capital firms and sharks swarm (pun intended). This is where shows like Shark Tank come into the investing process. Founders received what they can from friends and family fundraising (raises) or even skipped the process to go straight to their series A round of investing.

At this stage, due diligence becomes more serious. Lawyers are involved and the investor's team, if they have one, will run through your business with a fine-toothed comb. At this point, this book will guide you through the process, and help you prepare for meetings with your potential investors. You'll need to prepare to answer all questions and provide the correct documentation requested by the investor. If you acquire enough funding from different people, you'll have your due diligence process virtually on autopilot for the angels and VCs. In some cases, angels will only request the results and feedback from credible investors who have already went through due diligence with you. This saves both you and the investor time and money and can expedite receiving funds.

Your series C and D rounds of investment become even more serious as people look to acquire your company. Private Equity firms will solicit your interest to sell. Private equity firms, similar to venture capitalist syndicates, find people to put money into their company's fund with the hopes of receiving major returns to their investors. Private equity firms' goal is to beat the S&P 500 investment on a dollar by at least twenty percent. The difference for private equity firms is they own the company, work to grow profits before selling it to another private equity firm or going IPO (Initial Public Offering). After all, the most profitable part of startup investing happens when you, the company, sell or go public.

IPO is when your company becomes a publicly traded company on the stock market. Think of Apple, Inc. (AAPL), Amazon.com, Inc. (AMZN) or Microsoft Corporation (MSFT) as popular and now the largest IPO companies in history. Though we will not go into details of the IPO process, it's important to know the details related due diligence process increases significantly as a company works to have their own stock code on the New York Stock Exchange.

Big firms who do a lot of investments own "deal software" to simplify the due diligence process with you. It's an online software which makes it easier to collaborate and send/store documentation. Don't worry though, the process you create with the help of this book will overlap with the process of those firms.

After working with different investors and founders to write this book, each one had their own set of due diligence processes. The process you create after going through this book will easily overlay on top common steps and where the pieces need to fit, they will. The question is, "Are you ready to present your business to the masses?"

Corporate Structure

It may seem ridiculous to remind you, but before you go through the due diligence, you must have your business created legitimately with a state and the federal government. You must have a legal business and a business model prior to going to your first pitch meeting. There are workshops and information on all the different company structures and how to pick the right one for you so we will not go into those into too much details. Do you know how your company's structure will affect you as a founder or investor? Not all corporate structures are created equally, and yes, your company structure makes a difference to investors. We will review the company structure preferred by the highest level of investors.

Do not setup your corporate structure until you understand the tax ramifications. Reach out to an accountant to understand the liability you take by filing in each structure. If you have already set it up, don't worry, you can change your company structure at any time. There are a few main types of corporate structures to take into consideration when you're starting a business. You have to be the judge on what you want to do. Even if your investors want it to change, you're the CEO and you must decide for yourself.

Sole Proprietorships make up over seventy percent of the businesses in the U.S. Many people start businesses as a side hustle without having to register this way. Many do not even gather the fact they are sole proprietors. Unfortunately, these people are individually negligible in the investing world. A sole proprietor may receive the benefit of friends, family, and fools round, but it will not go any further. No serious investor in their right mind should invest into a sole proprietorship. There's too much liability as a founder and investor to move forward.

When sitting in a pitch with a startup founder, my investment group found out the founder, though they owned an LLC, mixed their personal and business funds across multiple accounts. The founder mismanaged their bank account to the point they closed several personal accounts and their business account became charged off. This is one reason (and a big ONE!) why investors do not think highly of sole proprietorships. It's difficult to track financials properly. If something happened to the founder, the business could not continue to run, and the tax benefits are non-existent if an investor tried to give the founder money.

A Limited Liability Company (LLC) shows a little more promise as beyond a friends, family, and fools round. This is where most young startups begin when they first file for their business structure. This is also the place where most novice investor begin because they're not sure what exactly to do or they're amenable to the startup being new. At this point, some angel investors and venture capitalists are willing to invest but cautiously. Larger VCs are reluctant to invest due to tax implications, but they may invest on the contingency of the company filing to become a C-Corp. It is difficult to sell or transfer membership and ownership of your company if it is an LLC.

S-Corporations (S-Corp) are outstanding structures, but it has some limitations. Investors outside of the United States cannot legally invest in an S-Corp. These corporate structures also limit investment to "natural person" and not companies. This means they restrict venture capital firms from being investors. Also, S corporations can only have up to 100 shareholders, and they can only distribute common stock, and not preferred stock.

C-Corporations (C-Corp) gives investors the all-access pass to investing. A popular move for a startup looking for funding is to register your business with the state of Delaware as a C-Corp. Yes, I said Delaware. In fact, more than 50% of all major companies in the United States incorporate in the state of Delaware[1]. If you look at the fine print or term and conditions of corporations like Google, you'll find them registered in Delaware. Founders register in this state because it is the most startup and business friendly state for business laws, rules, and regulations. Courts (The Delaware Court of Chancery) are extremely business friendly, and it commits them to resolve business cases quickly. Startups looking for large sums of funding have registered their business in Delaware. If they haven't, they likely have the paperwork ready to submit as soon as they receive their first nibble from an interested investor.

Once you have registered for your corporation, the next thing to do is have an Employee Identification Number (EIN). We also know this as the Tax Identification Number (TIN) or the Federal Employer Identification Number (FEIN). This is simple to do through www.irs.gov during standard federal business hours. Now you've legally formed your business, it's time to prepare to be operational.

Financial Foundation

Don't panic! No finance degree needed for this section. Let's review the basics. Fundamentally, investors want to know about your money and how you spend it. Unlike established companies however, this is not the most important part of investing unless you're talking about financial forecasts. Most startups at this stage are not making money, and if they are, it's not enough for an investor to become excited over. To run a successful business whether it be a startup or established business, there are things you need to operate.

A business bank account is a must and is one of the first steps to making your business operational. As soon as you establish your entity with the state, you will file for your EIN, then go directly to the bank and setup your business account. Today, you can create business bank accounts online which eliminates the need to go into a banking center.

Cutting corners by using your personal bank account will hurt you especially when going through the funding process. I've met a founder who created no accounting system and no business bank account. With everything tied together, there became no way to audit the financials he put together. Unfortunately, we didn't invest in his business though we thought the founder had a great business. Many founders make this mistake starting off, and it skews their financials when reviewing financial history.

With your bank account open, it's also smart to sign up for a business line of credit. I'm not here to give financial advice but treat your business credit as if it is precious cargo on your way to business success. Your business has its own credit identity and it should be treated separately than your personal credit but with the same respect. Many banks offer a business credit card, which helps build business credit. As a business, it's important to create business accounts with vendors you use often. If you use office supplies, you can go to Amazon, Office Depot/Office Max, or Staples to open an account with a line of credit. Companies such as FedEx and UPS do the same and it is a great option for companies shipping a lot of products. Having accounts such as these build a credit history for your company.

It's important your business builds financial strength. There are companies such as Dun and Bradstreet who rate the financial strength of your company from your credit score to how well your company would do under financial stress. Even while setting your company up, it would be wise to sign up for a Data Universal Numbering System (DUNS or D-U-N-S numbers). Dun & Bradstreet provides DUNS numbers for free and is one of the top business credit bureaus. Most financial institutions use your DUNS credit score to determine your creditworthiness when applying for a loan. Just as with your personal credit, Experian and Equifax also monitor your business credit. Unlike your personal credit, they do not always register your business and start tracking your company's credit history. You would have to go on each credit site to register it yourself. Investors can look at all your credit history and they'll likely ask for your DUNS number. If you're prepared and make wise credit decisions, no need to worry about this negatively affecting your funding process.

A friend of mine acquired a business back in 2007. She was extremely excited about this new venture and felt the company showed significant signs of success with a book of business. What she did not consider included the fact she was buying a business with no working capital. Before she knew it, she acquired $75,000 in credit card debit with her personal credit. Ten months later, her exciting and what seemed to be promising business closed. She asked her parents for $50,000 to pay back the loan and over 10 years later, she continues to pay off the debt. Poor financial decisions create hard lessons but ones you will never forget.

Financial Tracking

Having an accounting system is very important for your company and your due diligence team. As a founder, you should track all financials in one place to eliminate an additional room for error. Some founders find it easier to track their financials in excel spreadsheets. It's fine but not preferred by an investment team. Manual tracking creates additional opportunities for mistakes, typos, and the temptation to fudge the numbers as you see fit to win the investment. You will have to provide certain financial models to your potential investor up front, however there's a period of validation in which the due diligence team wants to go through the books themselves and do their own analysis. Larger businesses use Enterprise Resource Planning (ERP) Systems where all their data including finances, accounting, and purchasing is in one place. Larger investment firms (especially private equity firms) can and will opt to audit these systems for accuracy. Having all your information in one place provides a great convenience to your investors and your startup.

NOTE: I will not cover in great detail about financial documentation however I will cover what is important to an investor.

Your balance sheet is a report showing how much money is dedicated to your assets, liabilities, and owner's equity. Assets are the pieces of equipment you own. Assets could include cash on hand, property, equipment, or even insurance. Liabilities are commodities where you owe money. You may have purchased a property, yet you have a balance on the loan as part of your accounts payable. Owner's equity is the money left once you subtract your liabilities from your assets.

Cash Flow is very important for any business. For a startup looking for investment, it's not important for the reasons you may suspect. Investors want to see your cash flow to understand your burn rate more than your income. If the business's cash flow is positive, they are bringing in money. Most business who are cash flow positive are not looking for additional investment unless the cash flow is too low to keep up with business growth. The burn rate is the speed in which you are losing/spending money. If your cash flow is negative, you then have a burn. The burn rate of startups are calculated on a monthly basis and also helps the investor understand when you're going to run out of money. According to Brex.com[2], the average monthly burn rate for pre-seed startup is right under $18,000, for seed round startups, $75,000, just below $400,000 for Series A, $500,000 for Series B, and $900,000 for "graduated" series A startup companies. Yes, these dollar amounts are burn rates per month. At the early stages, a founder couldn't imagine spending $900,000 a month in expenses.

Profit/loss statements and income statements are not as important to an investor to invest in a startup. The reason you are searching for funding is because you don't have enough or no profit to put back into the business's growth. Most startups are at a loss month after month. The above two financial documents give the investor a better idea of what they are entering into as they invest in your business. A business with too much debt or an abnormally fast burn rate will throw up red flags for the savvy investor.

Documentation

Due diligence documentation is extremely important. This is the primary starting point for founders. I have met with many founders who could not find the correct information when asked to provide it. Not because they did not have it or they were trying to hide it, but because of no organization in how they documented and stored their business information. The best way is to store all your documents in a cloud storage with a backup. This gives you access to all your documentation from anywhere and keeps a backup in the event of data loss. The last thing you need is to be out of town, and you can't access the data requested by an investor or you damage your laptop while traveling containing all your business information. It has happened! I'll walk through how to best structure your information into file folders, then at the end of this chapter you can see the full structure for yourself. NOTE: There are different types of software that can replace these folders however to stay lean as a founder, having a standard online file folder structure is the most inexpensive approach.

Team Folder

Start with a Team Folder. This folder houses all the information about your current and past team members. It is also important to have information on members who have left the company. If you've ever watched television shows such as The Profit, Marcus Lemonis has a reputation of calling old employees back. An investor may do the same if you have key people who have left your startup. Each team member should have their own separate subfolder with information such as their background check results, a copy of their driver's license, passport, etc. You can also include the background check form they filled out and a copy of their declaration of minority status. Optionally, you could include summaries of any reference calls made when hiring each employee. Also, within this folder, have each of the team members' resumes. Include all your founder information in this folder too. The team folder should always be kept private to anyone other than the startup's leadership, HR, and founders.

Legal Folder

The second folder is your Legal Folder. All your information needed to keep the business up and running legally goes in this folder. This documentation includes your Articles of Incorporation you created to start your business. Your startup needs to have By-laws and an Operating Agreement (even if you're the sole member of the startup currently). Save any contracts and/or agreements in this folder. Even if an agreement has expired or became voided, keep them and any revisions in your Legal Folder. If you have set up your board of directors, include all documents related to meeting minutes, elections, stock purchasing, and issuance.

Intellectual Property Folder

A very important sub-folder to create within this your legal folder is information on intellectual property such as trademarks, patents, copyrights, and trade secrets. These are not typically shared with an investor upfront and sometimes not at all. Sharing trade secrets could be a major liability for a business, even if you want to share it with a "trusted" investor.

Market Folder

Create a Market Folder for your sales and marketing team. This does not contain ads and marketing material; this will go into your Commercial Folder. It contains documents related to show your market strategy and analysis. Include the product market fit, benchmarking analysis, and long-term market strategies. Just like in the Legal Folder, name all revisions consistently and archive in this folder.

Commercial Folder

Your Commercial Folder digs into your business-like roots of a tree. It's the heart of your business and how it works. This folder contains your one-page credit application, which is a capabilities statement telling what your business does. Also include your detailed business plan, business model canvas, lease agreements, work history for as long as you can go back (at least 3 years), and a list of equipment you lease and/or own. Your business plan includes your SWOT analysis, financial projections, core business processes, and sales and marketing material. The Commercial Folder serves as a place to show you have vetted your fundamental idea, created content around it, and received the proper licenses to do business and operate.

Technical Folder

Technical Folder is not just for tech companies. It holds demo videos and tutorials on how to use the startup's technology. It also has a continuous product roadmap showing how and when you plan to roll out fresh functionality into your product. If you do not have a technology business, the product or service roadmap can still apply.

If you are not implementing technology, your folder will hold information of the software and hardware you are using and any guides on how to use it. If you have custom software to run your business, an investor's team may need guidance on how to navigate the tool. The investment team will appreciate this information upfront.

Finance/Tax Folder

Finally, and most important, create a Financial/Tax Folder. This houses all financial information your investor will most likely ask for. In the structure and the end of this chapter, I provide the most commonly asked for examples, such as "Can you provide 2 years of tax returns and 12 months of bank statements."

As stated in the previous section, if you have the right technical accounting and finance systems such as an ERP, you can export most of this information out of your system in real time as the investor asks for it. If your business doesn't have long enough business history, an investor may ask for your personal financial statements and tax returns.

File Folder Outline

Below is the fundamental outline of what was mentioned earlier in this chapter. This will be your guiding structure to prepare for due diligence. If you do not have some information, keep the folders or subfolders for future use.

Team Folder (Main Folder)
1. Background checks (Subfolder)
    1. Birth certificates
    2. Driver's licenses
    3. Passports
    4. Declaration of minority status
    5. Reference calls
2. Resume of founders and key employees (Subfolder)

Commercial Folder (Main Folder)
1. One-page credit application
2. Business plan (Subfolder)
    1. Business model (Subfolder)
3. Business registrations
    1. Employee identification number
    2. DUNS number
    3. CAGE code
    4. Business license and permits
4. Sales and marketing material (Subfolder)
    1. Logo
    2. Marketing material
5. Processes (Subfolder)
    1. Process maps
    2. Client journey
6. Lease agreement (Subfolder)
    1. Security deed or homeowner's deed
7. Work history for 3 years (Subfolder)
8. Equipment list (Subfolder)

Market Folder (Main Folder)
1. Competitor analysis
2. Product Market Fit

1. Customer/Client references (Subfolder)
2. Long-term growth strategy (Subfolder)

Legal Folder (Main Folder)
NOTE: All necessary documents must be signed

1. Articles and Certificate of Incorporation
2. Bylaws
3. Partnership agreements (Subfolder if necessary)
4. Organizational and operating Agreements (Subfolder)
5. Vendor and client contracts (Subfolder)
6. Board meeting minutes (Subfolder)
7. Elections (Subfolder)
8. Stock purchase documents (Subfolder)
9. Letters of Intent (Subfolder)
10. Option issuance documents (Subfolder)
11. Employment agreements (Subfolder)
12. Investor agreements (Subfolder)
13. Intellectual Property (Subfolder)
    1. Trademarks
    2. Patents
    3. Copyrights
    4. Trade secrets

Financials/Tax Folder (Main Folder)
1. Past financials (Subfolder)
2. 2 years of tax returns (Subfolder)
3. Bank statements (Subfolder)
4. Current financials (Subfolder)
5. Financial projections (Subfolder)
6. A/R report (Subfolder)
7. Personal financial statement (Subfolder)

8. Profit loss and balance sheet (Subfolder)
9. Current and prior year cash flow statements (Subfolder)
10. Bank statement for the last 12 months (Subfolder)

Technical Implementation Folder (Main Folder)
1. Demo videos/instructions (Subfolder)
2. Product implementation roadmap (Subfolder)

Chapter Three: Rules of Engagement

What Kind of Investor Are You?

When becoming an investor, it is wise to first know the type of investor you are according to the SEC. The United States Securities and Exchange Commission (SEC) provides these guidelines. They are the federal body defining the requirements you need to meet for each category of investor. As of today, the three categories of investors include; the unaccredited investor, the accredited investor, and the qualified (or "sophisticated") investor.

If you're a new investor with little capital to invest you are likely an unaccredited investor. This doesn't mean they do not allow you to invest your money; it means they limit you in how and how much money you are allowed to invest. I started off as an unaccredited investor. Whether you're unaccredited or not, investing minimal amounts of capital starting off is a smart strategy.

Many people will take your money, however the old adage of "don't put all your eggs in one basket" is true if you're a novice or experienced investor. Diversifying your portfolio of businesses helps you reduce the risk of losing your money in one or two businesses. Spread your money around in hopeful startups and more established companies. Start off with one or two companies, learn from your experiences as an investor. As you become more comfortable with your role and expectations, you can impart your wants and needs to the future startups.

The long game for an investor should also include gaining credibility, finding a unicorn, and developing your own process of operation. The operation includes what is important to you as an investor. What process do you want to take a company through to vet them for your portfolio? Essentially, what are YOUR rules of engagement? As an investor, you hold most of the cards up front, meaning you can decide how this process is going to go.

Accredited Investors

Most investors strive to become an accredited investor. You meet the income or net worth requirements to obtain the rights and privileges of an accredited investor. At the time of writing this book, to qualify, you must meet at least one of the below criteria:

1. An Individual must have an income exceeding $200K for the past two years with a reasonable expectation the $200K threshold will be reached in the current year.
2. A married couple must have a joint income exceeding $300K for each of the past two years with a reasonable expectation the $300K threshold will be reached in the current year.
3. An individual or individual and spouse must have a net worth exceeding $1M. Here the net worth excludes the value of the individual's primary residence. Other residences can be included.

OR

An entity not considered a natural person (e.g., Equity Fund, Holdings Corporation) qualifies as an accredited investor if it meets at least one of these below criteria:

1. It owns at least $5M in assets.
2. All the owners of the entity are themselves accredited investors.

The SEC puts these requirements in place because they believe those who meet the required criteria can take the risk of investing in a such a high-risk investment vehicle (mainly startups but also real estate). To be clear, startups are failing at a rate of over seventy-five percent during the time of writing this. You don't want to lose your money at this same rate. As an accredited investor, the world of investing in startups is practically limitless. Meeting these requirements provides an individual or entity the ability to offer seed capital, private equity, venture capital, hedge funds, private placements, and equity crowdfunding contributions. On the other side of this coin, if you do not invest wisely, you could lose your entire fortune.

Do not feel discouraged if you do not meet any of these requirements. Only about two percent of Americans are eligible accredited investors. This leaves a small window for founders to find investors. The SEC combats the low number of accredited investors by also creating the categories of qualified investors and non-accredited (or unaccredited).

Qualified Investors

Many people interchange "accredited investor" and "qualified investor." By SEC definition, these are two different individuals or entities. Qualified investors are the super, mega, extremely sophisticated investors who have an investment portfolio of at least five million. Sophisticated investors may not have the net worth or income requirements, but they have the savvy to make sound investments. This portfolio of at least five million is money they manage, not necessarily their own money. Their professional experience "qualifies" them as people who make smart investments and have done so historically. These people or authoritative bodies could be corporate entities, wealth managers, investment bankers, institutional investors, or registered investment advisers (RIAs).

Unaccredited Investors

Unaccredited Investors could also invest in startups except most founders feel deterred to do so. Raising funds from an unaccredited investor incurs additional fees and paperwork. Even if a founder were to let unaccredited investors in, they are limited to only thirty-five unaccredited investors. Also remember, unaccredited investors provide less money to the founder's startup. A founder would rather target a small number of accredited investors who can provide greater capital than a larger number unaccredited investors who can provide less capital.

An option would be investing in partnership with an accredited investor or an investment firm. This is more effort for the unaccredited investor because you will have to find a firm who is willing to work with you. Also, there's additional paperwork needed to be filled out between the unaccredited investor and the firm.

Unaccredited Investors in Crowdfunding

The rules of engagement for an unaccredited investor is quite detailed through two major acts created by the SEC. The JOBS Act, also known as Jumpstart Our Business Startups Act, passed into law on April 5, 2012. This act protects novice investors, but at the same time it reduces a founder's potential of early growth through unaccredited investments. The JOBS Act focuses on crowdfunding which allows founders of startups to openly solicit investment from the public. This made the way for the surge in crowdfunding platforms such as Wefunder, Indiegogo, and Kickstarter. Crowdfunding has become extremely popular for non-accredited investors however there are other options for acquiring crowdfunding equity.

Crowdfunding is not limited to online marketplaces, crowdfunding for non-accredited investors applies to any kind of equity and real estate investment opportunities. Instead of putting money into a Kickstarter to receive the latest smart watch or robot, some platforms allow you to earn equity and other perks as an investor. Real estate crowdfunding offers several options on how and what you can invest. These options allow investors to further diversify their portfolio even if they want to focus on real estate.

Unaccredited Investors in Real Estate

You could invest in land. Developers often want to purchase large quantities of land to build communities, and they do not have the required capital. This is especially the case for new developers who have not established capital to expand into multiple areas simultaneously. There are some established developers whose business model is to use investors to acquire their land for development.

Another way to invest is providing contributions to the mortgage of a residential or commercial property. Through "flipping" properties, the common return on investment may come a lot faster. Once the property is renovated or upfitted, your return comes with the sale of the property. Investors can find real estate investment companies who will provide a prospectus of what the return may look like and how quickly it will sell as well as manage the work of flipping the home. This would be part of the pitch and due diligence. Your job as an investor is only to provide capital. The purpose of these firms who renovate and retrofit the properties is to create quick returns for themselves and potential investors.

On a similar note, real estate investment firms purchase properties, upfit and renovate them for the purpose of leasing the property.

As an investor, you should receive a similar prospectus which contains the potential monthly revenues a property could produce and the timeline for the property to start generating revenue. As an investor, you will receive recurring payments until the property is sold like you would from a startup. Also like a startup, the real money is in the sell.

If you want to focus strictly on real estate, you can participate in a real estate investment trust (REIT). REITs are companies who invest in commercial and residential real estate for the purpose of creating revenue. Like private equity funds, you as an investor can put your capital with a pool of other investors to create major buying power.

Many people do not know it but over eighty-five million[3] Americans invest in REITs through their 401K and other retirement vehicles. You can do this directly with the REIT, however. Investors like this option because they do not have to spend the time finding, buying, and managing the property. They also do not have to do all the financing or find other investors to help finance. Reputable REITs produce more stable possibilities of returns which is why so many financial services companies use them.

Unaccredited Investors in Lending

During the time of this book, micro-lending is a profitable yet time consuming source of revenue. As a micro-lender, you provide small sums of money (called micro-loans) to another individual with the expectation of receiving interest on the loan. This method of investing takes the banks, credit unions, and independent lending companies out of the picture.

Though this sounds like loan sharking, investors provide legitimate agreements and interest rate payments to the borrower.

Besides, there are laws to prevent you from being a loan shark with high interest rates and extreme repercussions for not making your payments on time. Now the target market for investors vary significantly. Investors choose who they want to invest in through their own due diligence criteria. It could be based on how the borrower plans to use the money, the region they live in, or their income levels.

Some investors have started microlending in countries who have little or no financial services options otherwise. This allows people to build businesses or pay for materials to build a home. Keep in mind microlending strategies, like startup investing, is about the long game. You would likely need to provide hundreds of loans to make six-figure returns.

Though there are a variety of ways for unaccredited investors to grow their money, the investment activities remain somewhat consistent. You should still complete due diligence. Now the process and criteria may not be the same if you're investing in real estate or a startup, you will still want to have a process. Due diligence is what makes the difference between high and low returns. It's up to you to buy-in to consistently and carefully making good investment decision.

Securities Act of 1933

Due diligence originated in the Securities Act of 1933. If brokers exercise the option to complete due diligence, the founder and broker are not liable for non-disclosure of information the investor did not discover. Due diligence is about taking "careful consideration" of a company which involves the practice of checking the details of claims made by its founder. The entrepreneur doesn't drive the due diligence process, it's on the investor. The investor possesses the right to ask for what they want to make a sound decision. It is then the founder's choice to provide the information. If they do not, they risk not receiving the investment but as stated before there is some information a founder should not provide.

To understand why due diligence is important and the right of an investor is to understand the JOBS Act and the Securities Act of 1933. In this book, the word securities refer to the buying and selling of equity ownership in a startup.

When I first learned about the Securities Act, I thought it to be absurd. Why would someone tell me how to spend my money? I first heard about this law in 2016 on episode 7 of the popular podcast, Startup, a mini-series about how Alex Blumberg started his famed podcasting business, Gimlet Media. At the time, the qualifications for an unaccredited investor still required you to be a wealthy person. I felt like one of his other listeners:

"It feels very frustrating. I mean I feel like I have an ability to manage my finances. Just seems sort of strange and patronizing for...it is a government agency right, the SEC? For a government agency to tell me that even if I feel that I can afford to do this in fact that's not okay and I'm not allowed to make that choice."

To date, the SEC rules for a non-accredited investor as it relates to crowdfunding opportunities is as follows:

The rules impose limits on the amount an investor can invest in all Title III crowdfunding offerings over a 12-month period. Investors with both an annual income and net worth of at least $100,000 can invest up to 10% of the lesser of annual income or net worth, but an investor's total investment across all Title III offerings may not exceed $100,000 in a 12-month period. Other investors can invest the greater of $2,000 and 5% of the lesser of annual income or net worth.[4]

In a world where people are making less and saving more, I hope to see these laws change soon. Read more about the Title III rules and regulations for investors and founders at www.afterthepitch.com/resources.

The Securities Act also states it is the founder's job to be fair and honest with investors and potential investors. Investors have the right, through the Securities Act, to be able to make sound investment decisions. Ethically, the founder should want to be considered a credible person who wants to keep the brand and trust of future investors. By not being open and honest to the investor they're working with, it can be a hinderance for the founder to obtain future funding. The startup investing world is small and if a founder is considered to be deceitful, the word will travel quickly.

The Securities Act of 1933 protects the investor from being fraudulently deceived by a business. The definition of an investor is supposed to be re-evaluated every four years to make sure the market and economic conditions keep an investor safe. Many people I speak with do not like this law. As media exposure increases for startups searching for capital, more individuals are attracted to investing their money to diversify their portfolio. These same people do not qualify as accredited investors but have "disposable income" to help a startup founder and diversify their own portfolio. Lobbyist and consumer advocates believe the excitement around startups may cause tens of thousands of investors to move away from traditional investing, lose their money due to poor investment decisions, and cause the market to crash.

The SEC limits unaccredited investors (those who could cause the market to spiral into an abyss) the ability to invest in these companies but telling them how much and when to invest their money.

I didn't start out as an accredited investor, so I worked with a team of people who were able to add investment power to the capital I inserted into my startup. This is a testament about building your network. Some reputable investment groups offer slots for unaccredited investors to put in capital. It's your job to find those companies. However you decide to invest, remember your network is the most valuable resource you have. This text only provides a high level view for those investors who are not experts in this area. I encourage you to read in detail the laws related to investing.

Being an Investor

Becoming an investor is like being an entrepreneur. You create a bond with your partners when you invest. You're starting a new business venture. This process takes you through the same emotional roller coasters with the founder. The worst part is you're doing this numerous times with multiple businesses. Every new business brings different people, cultures, founders, and more importantly different roadblocks.

Depending on how you evaluate your business, you can experience the loss and failure of a startup (more importantly your money) if you do not complete thorough due diligence. It's like loaning someone money you barely know. My father always told me never to loan money to anyone if I expected repayment. If I didn't expect to (or need to) get my money back, then I wouldn't be as disappointed when I didn't. If I did expect to get it back and didn't receive if, I'll likely lose a relationship from it. People lose a lot in a relationship over money. The same is true with startup investing except you have an opportunity to increase your chances of repayment.

Investing creates a whirlwind of trials and successes. I've learned a lot about myself on this journey. Investing is more than providing startup capital. The best part about becoming an investor for me is learning your skills, honing those skills, and being a student of the craft of investment. The only way you're going to become a successful investor is by having the right team and appropriate knowledge to make a sound investment decision. Here are some prime characteristics I've seen in successful investors. How many characteristics do you have? Be honest with yourself.

Patience. Patience is a characteristic EVERY investor must have, or at least a moderate level of patience. Even though you'll work with lean startups who deliver quickly and grow just as quickly, it doesn't mean your returns will come quickly. Some startups do not provide a return for several years. When I first became an investor, I invested in a company gaining momentum and onboarding their first customers. I quickly realized the traction they were gaining did not equate to me receiving a return. They were obligated to pay people, put money back into the company as operating expenses, and hire more employees because of growth. Also, they needed additional cash on hand for emergencies. Though money was coming in, it wasn't coming out...and into my pockets.

You'll need additional patience if you are an active investor. As an active investor, you invest your time and knowledge into the business. This allows you to see the day-to-day operations, drive the direction of the company, and add more value than just capital. Being an active investor also means you experience the highs and lows of the company which will test your level of patience, especially during the lows. Patience also includes the ability to stay persistent during a loss and failure which are two activities guaranteed to happen to all serious investors on their journey.

Ability to accept loss. You will have some losses. Every serious investor does. There are parts of business no startup or investor can control no matter how great the idea or how much money they spend. Losing money can be a big ordeal for a new investor but it comes with the territory. You accept the risk for high returns. No one is exempt from losing money on an investment. It will happen to you.

Ability to accept failure. Failure also comes with the territory. You will fail yourself, your founder, or a potential founder who claims to own a great idea. Many investors are also entrepreneurs themselves. They become busy in the many activities they work on and it becomes overwhelming at times.

We all drop the ball sometimes, but we must brush ourselves off and try again. I've admitted to people many times I did not follow-up with a potential founder. Investors don't always follow through. Some founders shake their heads in agreement with this statement. We're not bad people. Life changes, we can constantly be pulled in many directions and some of us own our own business(es).

High tolerance for risk. I'm not a gambling man...well, maybe I am, since this is what I do. I take gambles on business ventures. Most of the ventures I've invested in do not have a product or service available to be sold. I invest extremely early because I can see the long-term vision and I can increase my chances of buy-in later rounds of a successful startup.

Your decision to invest is risky whether it be in startups or any other markets. There will be times you encounter an opportunity where the potential reward is just as high as the risk. You cannot avoid risks in this industry.

Ability to have a long-term vision. Long-term vision is vital. Whether it's provided to you by the founder or if it's your own vision, you must understand how you'll arrive there. I suggest you create a three-year vision for each investment. Five years is also good, but your vision and strategy start to become blurry at this point. With technological advances, it's difficult to project changes after year five.

Strong temperament. With accepting loss and failure and having a high tolerance of risk, an investor must have a strong temperament. It's advantageous to the investor to stay calm, positive, and continue to move forward with other opportunities when a business closes. This is difficult to do. You put time and money into a project to see it all vanish. You think of what you could have done different and times where you could have spoken up when you saw something wrong, but you let the founder handle it.

I find many investors possess a level of assertiveness and directness which can be on the border of being considered rude. Usually rudeness is not their MO, they are vested in the opportunities they have and want to see the return they expect. The best way to get that return is through having a sense of urgency in making the startup successful. If an investor comes to a founder questioning why a deadline was missed by a day, it's not because they're jerks, it's because they expect excellence out of their business and that's the best way to be successful.

Strong financial foundation. Of course, you need the excess capital to invest. New investors' success rates with startups range between fifty percent and ninety percent (depending on level of experience and tolerance for risk). Losing tens of thousands of dollars can be a blow to those who cannot afford to lose large sums of money. We've already spoken about the categories of investors but any type can feel a blow to their bank account depending on their financial foundation. My father always told me to never lend someone money if I expected to be paid back. Today, I still live by this policy with both people and investments. If I cannot afford to lose my excess cash, I will not invest in a startup. I also know I will do my part to make sure I get my money back.

Other than having the money, you should have a strong knowledge of financial metrics. You may not be able to analyze every data point or create your own financial projections, but you still need the ability to read simple balance sheets, cash flow, and profit loss statements. Learning how to read a detailed pro forma helps as well. Not only should you know how to read these documents; you need to know how to interpret them. Financial documents are like short mystery story books. They take you on a journey usually leaving room for interpretation and questions.

After reviewing these documents, ask a lot of why's.

- Why is there a decrease here?

- Why is there an increase here?
- Why are were your expenses so high during this month?
- Why is there so much burn and where is it coming from?
- Why do these liabilities exist and how do you plan to mitigate them?
- Why can't you lower cost here?
- Why did you decide to incur this cost to run the business?

The list of questions can go on and on. You, as an investor, need to know how to read and interpret the basic financial documents before having your financial team analyze them. It will save you and your team time and effort if you find something wrong early in the process. By having these basic skills, you become the first line of defense in preventing going through weeks of due diligence.

Interpersonal skills. Like it or not, you're going to have to work with people. I'm not saying you must be a socialite, but a good understanding of people is essential. The investors I interviewed have an uncanny ability to hold an engaging conversation and influence people. Some say investors talk a little too much, but I will leave the opinion to you. Their influence isn't because of their money or power, their influence comes from their knowledge. Founders and their peers consider the words they speak the gospel and because of their confidence in those words, people desire to be more like them.

I found myself enthralled in their business acumen. Had I not known better, they could have told me one hundred percent of businesses succeeded, and I would have believed them. They understand people and how they think.

I've heard some of them use Neuro-Linguistic Programming (NLP) as a primary way of fostering influence. Don't worry if you naturally do not have this skill, there's information online and in books. Go to www.afterthepitch.com/resources you can find more information on how to use NLP for influence.

Self-control. Temperament and self-control work together to make a good investor. There will be a constant level of interactions with all types of people. Keep control of yourself emotionally as well as physically.

I've only heard of one investor arguing in a pitch meeting to the point they almost fought. You must always obtain self-control. If you're an active investor, there may be times where debates become heated and you as the investor need enough self-control to keep all parties calm.

Willingness to learn. Knowledge is your key to open doors in the investment world. By gaining the right business acumen and diving face first into learning about certain industries, you'll find more founders and more investors who are interested in working with you. Don't be afraid to learn from other investors. They will amaze you at their level of knowledge in their industries. I often inquire of other investors when I'm considering a deal in another industry where I have limited knowledge. Leverage your resources and learn all you can.

Ability to teach. In the same vein of learning, be well versed to teach. You'll never know when you're on the other end of the investor call and a fellow investor asks you for some domain knowledge. Work diligently to know about the industry and be able to teach it, even if not required.

Many times founders are new to business. Your aptitude for business is usually what allows you to reach a higher level of investor respect and status. You have your own abilities and knowledge to bring to the table, so let it be fruitful to help others multiply.

Love and respect for entrepreneurs and startups. The lives of entrepreneurs and startups are difficult. There's plenty of late nights (I'm currently writing this section of the book at 2:00a.m.) where they're up working on their business. They sacrifice time with friends and family to pursue their dream.

If they're a single founder, it's even worse. They're going through the pain and success alone. They don't have anyone as invested as they are into their business, yet they still keep pushing forward. Granted, they may have friends, family, or advisers, but they are not in the trenches of the business with the founder.

Entrepreneurs are a special breed of people. Ones who would rather suffer through short-term pain to receive long-term gain. They are individuals who are visionaries and have passions they refuse to let go. Yes, it may sound or look crazy, but these people do what the majority won't do to achieve their version of happiness. It is ALWAYS good to love and respect this kind of determination!

My Advice to The Investor Reading This

Of all these characteristics, the important ones below have proven to create investment opportunities for myself.

- Teaching/mentoring ability
- Domain expertise
- Business experience
- Financial savvy
- Personal networks

My advice to you is to understand as much as possible about investing. Find investors in your area and ask if you can buy them lunch to learn about their process. There will be investors who will not give you the time of day, but there's plenty more who would love to offer you some advice on how to invest properly.

We are a part of a larger community where knowledge is best shared. We all have the same intent on increasing our knowledge, growing our startups to be successful, and receiving major returns.

As a first-time investor or one considering investing, don't be naive. If you want to become a serious investor, you will lose money. It happens, get over it. If you have ten thousand dollars of excess capital, do not pour it into one company. Spread it across multiple startups. Vet your startups as thoroughly as you can.

You may not have a team yet, but you may have friends or trusted advisors with business acumen who can help you where there may be gaps. Ask all the questions you need to until you're comfortable with handing your money over to what could be a stranger.

Also remember every founder possesses the "greatest new idea" having the "potential" to make millions or billions. Every founder tells a similar story whether they end up growing a successful company or one who will be out of business within the next year. By honing in on your skills based on this chapter, you'll have the ability to make the right decision the first time.

Chapter Four: Lessons From Investors

Not Everything Is Perfect

Leave your rose-colored glasses in the drawer, because your plans will not always turn out as intended. Don't let me discourage anyone from seeking funding or becoming an investor, but you need to know the good and bad.

My goals came from setting reasonable expectations. If I walked into this journey wearing rose-colored glasses expecting everything I did and every startup I worked with to provide excellent returns, I would end up disappointed. Even after going through strong due diligence, I never know what will happen.

I've met many founders who were on the verge of acquiring an investment or the startup they invested was on the cusp of being sold, when a company like Amazon or Verizon offers the same product or service. This almost immediately takes a chunk of the startup's market share potential and puts them out of business. As an investor and founder, unfortunately you can't predict the future and this is a risk you are taking on when you are in the startup world.

In other cases, I've seen companies pass through due diligence and another investor with way more money offers more money at an increased valuation. This causes the value of your dollar to go down and you must decide if you want to increase your investment, take less equity, or bow out to find another founder looking for capital. What will always stay true is if people know you are an investor, you will not have a shortage of founders reaching out to you asking if they can take your money. As an investor, remember your own value as you receive a barrage of requests to pitch. Author Russell Nohelty said, "Not every idea is meant to be made. Ideas are like petulant children, they will demand your attention." Same goes for investments and startup ideas.

To help you, the investor, my peers provided me with some hard lessons they learned as new investors and from other investors. At the request of a few, I removed their real name and company name. The nine stories from my associates will aid you with learning the right characteristics, mindset, and important lessons of investing.

9 Common Mistakes Made By New Investors:

Story One: Investing without Due Diligence

I met Jane Georges in 2010, a former WNBA basketball player who commands the room, and besides being six foot seven inches tall, you wouldn't think twice about her playing for the WNBA. People instantly notice her. The confident figure in the room who doesn't play games (no pun intended) as she struts confidently in her pressed light grey pantsuit.

Jane, only 37 years old, places herself in a predominantly older white male industry. Being around wealthy men doesn't bother her though, she seems to be used to it or just doesn't care. Everyone knows her because she made it a priority to connect with the right people in the room. When she approached my colleague and I at this meeting, it became apparent she loves the game of investing as much as the game of basketball.

At the time Jane invested in three companies, her portfolio comprised her two areas of expertise, electronics and sports. Her top three picks were strong and with her being one year into all three, the word "abnormal" would be an understatement when talking about their traction. I came to know her from joining conversations other investors held with her.

Though she possesses a direct and to the point attitude, she boldly shares her passions for startup companies and their founders. She takes care of them, but more importantly, she takes care of the people she likes in the investors' community.

When she walked up to us, she immediately inquired about us wanting to know who we were, did we have kids, were we married, and how were we liking the event. Even though she wasn't the host she made us feel comfortable.

Once she asked about our portfolios (which I deemed mine non-existent at the time), her eyes lit up at my colleague's portfolio and my interest in becoming an investor. We ended up finding seats in the ballroom's corner and talked for over an hour before parting ways. She helped me with my investment strategy and I'm still grateful for the advice to this day. She offered to bring me in on a deal if it included my main strength. I felt like I created a plan and left just as excited as she did when we told her we were new investors. Well, at least I was the rookie.

Jane showed genuine passion, yet when I ran into her years later, she told me a great story about her fourth business investment. This startup existed outside her wheelhouse, but she took on the initial investor meeting. The device will "shake up the food and beverage industry" the founders told her. They pulled her so far on the hook they closed the deal with one of those "limited-time offer" pitches you hear at car dealerships. Not only did they present her with a demo and hand her a product to take home, they gave her the option of reopening the round temporarily to jump in at a better valuation before increasing it.

She made an executive decision. One of those executive decisions she would be terminated for if she were working for a Fortune 500 company. She invested without going through a due diligence process!

For any current investor reading this, you're saying, "NOOOOOOO!" in the back of your mind. She developed an excellent due diligence process and my first meeting with her reminded me of the importance of having a process and using it consistently creates a successful business.

Months later she went against her own advice and made the worst mistake in her career. She felt pressured by the founders to write the check before they left the room. Even though she possessed business savvy, the idea seemed great. Their financials looked good, the founders were in sync with one another, and FOMO reared its ugly head.

She did not know the company began burning through more money than necessary. They were desperate for more capital and this happened to be their last-ditch effort to keep their business alive! The effort worked for them, but not their company.

Jane ended up suing them for providing false information. Though she received her money…eventually, she never invested without going through her due diligence process. Jane asked about the financials and they knowingly provided her false documentation. Doing this is probably the only way she won her case. Her choice not to go through due diligence by her own omission resulted in a loss of time and money.

Story Two: Creating A Long Due Diligence Process

I met Jared McConnell in 2008, and we reconnected before I decided to write this book. People knew him as a shy guy until he graduated from college. He spent his first few years out of college traveling on his dad's fortune and came back to work at an insurance company. This led him to falling in love with money management and helping people grow their financial legacy. I thought of Jared as smart and many people could tell he loved his work. He broke out of his shell in this industry and almost overnight became the city's socialite.

Jared's father invested in the Mergers and Acquisitions (M&A) sector for large corporations, but held little knowledge about the startup world. His father's advice came from love, but created a painful financial lesson for Jared. M&A due diligence and startup due diligence are two unique processes. Jared's determination to complete his due diligence process, M&A style, became a long, drawn out process and proved unsuccessful with his first investment.

Jared's story is not unique, because every new investor wants to make sure the decision to invest is a sound choice. He became a very analytical investor after working as a high net worth financial advisor for a well-known Fortune 500 company. His education and experience compelled him to do thorough research to help make the right decisions for his clients. His values and consistency make him a great advisor and he felt it would help him in the startup world.

A financial technology (fintech) company became the first startup to catch his eye, because he loves the fintech space. He completed tons of research and joined a few organizations around the fintech space. With his computer science degree, he thought he could still add a lot of value if he found the right startup for him. During a pitch breakfast with a new startup founder who already garnished traction, Jared approached the founder, and they both agreed working together interested them and started the due diligence process.

Jared developed his team, his advanced Microsoft Excel spreadsheets with formulas and micros, and his 200-point due diligence checklist. I may be over or under-estimating the points, but you catch my drift. Only a vehicle inspection sheet should be this long.

His checkoffs contained checkoffs as well as second opinion checks and rechecks.

He checked off every check except for writing the check. Eight months into the due diligence when Jared described the process as "just about halfway done," the founder decided his process wasn't worth the trouble. He informed Jared he planned to look for other investors who could help streamline company processes, not create more work for his team. The startup went on to be extremely successful and ended up being sold for $500 million four years later.

Jared is still kicking himself over the deal but has since changed his processes to help his company decide within 180 days.

Story Three: Investing Without A Legal Team

I've been grateful to have a holistic team of investors. We have investors who understand sales, marketing, legal, data, financials, technology, and real estate over a wide range of industries. Without them, I would struggle to put the right team of non-investors together to make the right decisions. Your due diligence team is crucial to your success as an investor. If you're an angel investor you may not have a team, but I suggest you have one key member on your due diligence team. A business lawyer will save you from disaster.

No one I've met understands the importance of a lawyer more than Rohon Lee. Rohon's journey didn't start with the expectation of becoming an angel investor. Rohon thought he wanted to be a serial entrepreneur. He sold two businesses for over $80 million dollars. He co-founded a tech startup in college and in his senior year sold it for $82 million dollars. The second startup he sold for an undisclosed amount, but he confirmed to me the amount hovered over $100 million.

Rohon is inconspicuous. If you find him at an event, he's like the guy standing in a corner people watching with a watered-down cocktail in his hand. His perfectly spiked black hair, tailored shirts with his initials, and Konstantino cufflinks shows he like nice things but his slight over-sized suit covers up the initialed cuffs and makes him look more like a college student than a millionaire.

With his two businesses sold, he lost his core team. His lawyers, finance gurus, and his business development teams were gone. With the talk of his transition into angel investing, he received a flood of calls and emails from Canadian startups (Quebec City is his hometown). He understood the due diligence process and felt he could go it alone without his trusted teams. He met with five companies during three months and worked on due diligence for each. This is what I would call a mistake if you're a single investor who invest large sums of money with no team. However, he became successful at completing his due diligence in a timely manner.

Of those five startups, he picked one. He used a combination of templates from his past two startups and sent it to the founders for agreement. Surprising to him, the founders signed the agreement, delivered it back over to him by morning, and sealed the deal.

No negotiation? Leaving the deal table with no negotiation is unusual. It's almost unheard of for a startup not to negotiate the equity to their advantage (unless already stated the deal would be a firm offer upon completion). He and the founders discussed no prior agreements. Rohon let it go and moved on.

A year later, Rohon finally brought on a lawyer and developed a complete investment team. While reviewing past contracts, the lawyer noticed an inconsistency in the informal communications and the term sheet provided to the founders. The lawyer realized Rohon made a typo and valued the company higher than originally agreed upon. This meant he owned a much smaller equity stake in the business.

Rohon almost suffered a mental breakdown but then realized there's nothing he could do to change his mistake. If he had let a qualified lawyer read it first, his investment would be secure and his return much higher.

Develop your team and do not shortcut the process. Don't be that person!

Story Four: Accepting a High Valuation

Speaking of valuations and teams, Hogan Starnes experienced a similar challenge. Named after the popular WWE Champion Hulk Hogan, he did not look like his namesake although he garnished enough muscular build to see he regularly attended the gym. At forty he is already balding. To make up for his hair challenges, he dresses in the latest men's formal fashion. Most of the time he is one of the youngest people in the room, but you can't tell. Hogan blends in and stands out all at the same time.

He also did not have a team or a strong financial foundation. Hogan is a peer of mine who I originally felt the need to emulate when I decided to become an investor. Though widely known in many financial circles with new and seasoned investors. He talked a better game than he played. He joined the ranks of some of the finest investors though he never invested. In his late thirties he took the plunge.

He went through a dozen or more investor meetings with founders to come up empty-handed before or after due diligence. Finally, a good friend of Hogan's introduced him to a company founder whose startup specialized in expediting the wine and spirit making process.

The machinery seemed innovative to Hogan. Being able to age wine in a week versus two to three years by doing it naturally seemed to solve a major need for the wine and spirit businesses. Hogan considered it a great technology and to his knowledge, no one had tried this method in the industry.

Just because no one has tried a technology or idea does not mean another company, whether it be a large corporation or another startup, is not working on the same technology or idea. It also doesn't mean it's an excellent idea. Even if your startup is the first to market, there will ultimately be copycats if you gain traction.

There were two mistakes Hogan made on this deal. First, he possessed no knowledge of this industry and didn't take much time to learn about it before deciding to invest. Second, the valuation of the company appraised too high at such an early stage of investment.

The founders completed the technology but never fully tested it. The science and theory were correct, but the startup did not know if their machine could withstand the mass production and multiple uses. Guess what? It couldn't.

The product ended up being a dud despite the founders putting an astronomical valuation on it.

Hogan thought the valuation made sense. He could have known better with the guidance of a team to tell him otherwise. He ended up investing more money to have the company go out of business six months later.

Story Five: Investing After Your First Pitch

Remember, IF YOU ARE NEW to investing, do not feel every investment is the right investment. Do not feel you are obligated to invest in a company because the founder is friendly, or it just sounds like a good idea.

There are a lot of ideas out there, and you have options. If you make a sound decision, great, but the first company presenting themselves to you is likely not the company for you to invest.

This is the case for many reasons. When you have your first investor's meeting, it's exciting. Everyone is at the table excited as well. The founder may have a sound and professional pitch, and all seems good in paradise.

If you have never been in any other investor meetings with other investors, you won't realize this magnifies the excitement. Which magnifies your desire to invest. Remember, you must wet your feet before jumping into the middle of the ocean. Making a big financial decision before getting experience is detrimental. If you're investing with someone with investing experience, this theory is void.

After you meet more companies, it can become repetitive and sometimes discouraging. Don't base your decision on excitement, but your own qualifications and your preferences in the companies. Gaining experience takes hearing pitches and understanding different industries. Investing in the first company is usually an emotional decision more than a financial business decision. Because of this, investing in the first company that approaches you could be a bad idea. Financial decisions usually include you wanting to spend the money quickly because you have it or you feel this is the only opportunity you will receive for a return. Bes Bovell possesses first-hand knowledge of how emotional investment decisions lead to pain and heartache. Bes's parents immigrated to the United States over 50 years ago. They started their first dry cleaning business which expanded into other dry cleaners, several laundromats and two corner stores.

Entrepreneurship is all Bes knew so it became no surprise when he started his first business in high school. Bes became successful and he built a massive home, moved his now elderly parents in and took over the family businesses. Bes is what we call a mogul. His custom suits, Patek Philippe watches, his McLaren P1, Lamborghini Sesto Elemento, or Ferrari LaFerrari Aperta might be a sign he's done well with his career. Still, Bes is only in his mid-forties and looks kind of like a young Johnny Depp with a slight French accent.

Bes knew he possessed capital, and the risk and reward mentality he grew up with in a business family made him want to jump at angel investing. When the chance arose, he jumped in head first.

A founder presented an idea to help people spend less time in laundromats but spend more money.

Seemed like a great idea to Bes. He felt he could expand and buy less equipment, a smaller space, and increase his customer base by moving people in and out (a new value-add). Unfortunately, Bes skipped the chance of doing proper due diligence or looking close enough at the business model at the current landscape of the industry.

Bes never purchased a laundromat, only operated them. They were in the business so long they were almost running self-sufficiently. If he did the right due diligence, he would see the actual cost of this new technology. It would only make a new laundromat slightly more profitable. Existing laundromats would lose money because the cost of conversion, space, and upkeep were minimal. With this new product, maintenance costs were higher, and the buildings would hold unnecessary space. Selling washers and dryers wouldn't even have been lucrative enough to keep owners in business. Bes, however, jumped at the first opportunity only three weeks after he decided to invest. He lost his money on the investment.

EVERYONE WANTS YOUR MONEY! Do not be desperate, be smart. The opportunities will avail themselves to you.

Story Six: Not Having Reserve Capital

I invested in a group of founders I met in a conference some years back. They sat in the tech space, but I found myself in a very new industry (I feel like it still is). After many meetings and going through due diligence, I finally invested with my angel group. It seemed to be a solid investment and a good deal. We invested early; the founders knew the industry and developed a long-term roadmap to implement and upgrade their product. My type of business!

I chose not to put much capital into any business except my own. I did however strongly believe in this company and its founders.

Before my group signed on the dotted line, I went in with them. I felt good about it. A few months later, they came back asking for an additional injection. We did it with little hesitation. I went out to their office to see their progress, reported back and we completed the deal.

What I learned and almost made a mistake on is building a reserve. If I invest in an early stage startup, I should keep some additional money to the side for the next round of investing. You should do this for two major reasons. In the first round of funding the founder will probably incentivize you to add more capital. This is great for you because you may receive additional equity with little effort. Also, serious founders are looking to go round for round in their investment journey. If you do not add more capital, this will dilute your stake in the company. Yes, your percentage ownership can and likely will go down if you do not invest more money later.

All smart founders go back to early investors before going on a pitching tour. If you're in a location where there's little capital being invested in startups, you hold better cards than the founder who raises capital from outside investors.

You must make a choice. If the company is worth it, make sure you have additional funds to invest. If you're not sure about the company, maybe it's an excellent time to move on to your next pitch.

This is the best tip I can provide founders other than 'diversify your portfolio'. Having money set aside to provide a startup when they need additional capital helps you build more credibility. It's really a minor benefit other startups look at (or should look at) when choosing an investor. As a founder, if my investor has enough capital to inject more money, they're likely to make better decisions, offer better guidance, and work for the interest of my long-term growth versus an immediate need for a return.

Story Seven: Investing in Immediate Gains, Not Long-Term Vision

When someone approaches me telling me they want to be an investor, four out of five times, the reason is along the lines of "to make a lot of money in a little amount of time." Knowing how often startups fail puts it in perspective. Newbies with less experience in business should expect to lose their money faster than they gain it at first.

Each investor I know has their own formula to determine the right investment. Jim and Kayla Livingston are impressive examples of this. Jim and Kayla married and started their relationship as cofounders in a real estate company. Jim is your low-key guy, who very seldom speaks in front of groups and prefers to stay in the back of the crowd, far, far back in the crowd. When talking with him one-on-one, you see his passion for business and his excitement when you mention winter sports. His wife gave me a heads up on it being the key to unlocking his introversion box. He knew many famous competitors in skiing, bobsledding, the skeleton, ski jump, snowboarding, the biathlon and the other nine winter sports held at the Olympics. He also knew most of the rules of each game.

Kayla graduated from law school. She faced a hard time finding a job but finally found a place in real estate law. This led to her passion to buy homes. Kayla is outspoken and gregarious. People remember Kayla because of her friendliness and her ability to make you feel special. She makes most people feel like they were elementary school friends. Her ability to connect with people is almost hypnotizing. A trait I need to learn as an introvert myself.

Jim and Kayla experienced success in mostly flipping homes until the stock market went belly up. Though they sat on some properties for long-term investment, they knew with the market facing a downturn; they needed to find investment opportunities in other places. They looked toward startup investing. They looked at startups they felt could survive during the recession and create opportunities for fast and long-term returns.

Their desire to invest led to them on a startup shopping spree. Before they knew it, they invested in twelve companies over five months. A year went by and they only received a small return from two of the companies. Six companies ended up failing within the first year of investment because many other investors didn't see the "recession proof" qualities of the startup. The angel investment returns they were receiving from the startups were nothing compared to the 5-7 month gains they received in the real estate market. Startup investing is a long-term play if you want to be successful and build credibility.

Story Eight: Investing in An Uncapped Convertible Note

To better understand Jarvis' story, I included the basics of a convertible note.

A convertible note is essentially a loan provided by an investor for your business. At a pre-specified time, the investor can turn the loan amount into an equity stake in the startup's business. They express their "option" to convert the loan only if the startup is doing well. There are two types of convertible notes; capped and uncapped convertible note.

A capped note says if the investor decides to express their option, they will base the equity amount received by the investor on the original valuation of the company. This allows the investor to know what his option equity amount will be.

Conversely, an uncapped convertible note does not provide the investor with a valuation. The founder may want this because they do not know the valuation of the business at this point. It's in the best interest of the founder to want an uncapped option. This allows them to change the valuation based on other investments.

This is a horrible idea for an investor to take unless you have an MFN (Most Favored Nation) clause in the agreement of your convertible note. The MFN makes it fair in the case other investors come in with the expectation of diminishing the equity percentage of the initial investor(s) who took the uncapped convertible note. With this clause, the investor's capital injection can be converted at the same valuation as the new investor.

Jarvis Fox knows all about convertible notes. In fact, he's so savvy in this area most of his investments are some form of a convertible note. Jarvis used to be quite a big guy. He always made people laugh and usually grabbed everyone's attention. Unfortunately, his life changed when his doctor diagnosed him with cancer. He lost well over 100 pounds and though he always seemed to keep his spirits up, he became more of a recluse only coming out for some investment meetings and pitches. Most of the time he accepted pitches virtually with his syndicate group.

Jarvis has enough cash flow to be called up by any three of his favorite private equity funds to invest in a new company here or there. He possessed a subtle yet powerful method to name dropping. You would think he traveled to every place in the world and met every person possible.

For many years, Jarvis invested money for high net worth clients. He learned the game and the people early in his career. When he landed a famous baseball player as a client, his career skyrocketed to more high net-worth clients. When he learned about startup investing he jumped on the opportunity and has been doing it to this day.

One of his first investments consisted of an online chat company similar to Google Chat except with more robust features. The founder didn't want to part with equity right away as they were working to estimate the company's worth (or valuation). Jarvis accepted the convertible note, but an uncapped convertible note.

Though Jarvis knew what an uncapped convertible note entailed; he did not read the agreement carefully. It was a clerical error by the contracts team. Another lesson to consider, read the agreement thoroughly before signing. He skimmed over the agreement assuming it was just like any other agreement he signed. The agreement however possessed a significant change.

Months later, Jarvis read the agreement and without hesitation went to his legal team working to figure out a way to prevent the inevitable. How could he convert without having his shares diluted? By this time, the founders gathered more funding from other investors. It's still unknown if any of the other investors signed for an uncapped convertible note.

He wanted to ensure this mistake didn't happen again. He researched the ramifications of opting for a convertible note and his rights as an investor.

Since then he's preferred convertible notes, with other terms than the one with the online chat company. To date, Jarvis's angel portfolio consists of 74% convertible notes with the remainder being straight equity deals.

Story Nine: Not Properly Diversifying Your Portfolio

My favorite tip to investors is to diversify your portfolio. What does "diversify your portfolio" mean exactly? Should you invest in all types of business, or should you invest in a lot of business? Should you invest in many industries even if you do not know about some of them? Should you invest for the sake of building your portfolio? Diversifying your portfolio is not an art or science, it's all about consistency and playing the long game.

Now the number of companies you invest in is very important. Many investors say the sweet spot is twenty companies. Please go beyond this number. Twenty companies may sound like a lot but remember, you're an investor who is doing this as a career, not a hobby. If you are, consider working toward the twenty mark. Honestly, I haven't reached twenty yet. When I do, I will celebrate and you're invited. Mark my words! The words from a stingy investor.

Scott Holmes' financial legacy began with his great-grandfather who started several manufacturing businesses. The businesses and family wealth were so massive they created a "family office" to manage their money and assets. Though all of Scott's family ate and slept manufacturing, he went a slightly different route from his granddad and great-grandfather. Instead of starting new manufacturing companies as his family did, he gained an equity stake in innovative companies and created his own empire.

Scott used the knowledge he possesses from growing up in the family business. He's also been able to use the connections he and his father have made in the manufacturing world to grow the startups he invests. This helps startups gain traction quicker. Therefore, he can ask for a great percentage of a company outside of the money he injects into the startup. You may have seen similar discussions on *Shark Tank* about additional equity for domain knowledge and connections. Scott plays the role of more of a consultant who possesses an equity stake in the businesses. Not a terrible deal!

Manufacturing became his passion and he didn't want to move away from this industry. Scott did not predict the hard hit to his portfolio during the 2008 recession. The recession cut his manufacturing revenues. Sales slowed in literally all the markets his companies manufactured. He possessed no way to bounce back from the losses. Most of his companies manufactured basic materials like paper, office supplies, concrete, and vehicle parts. All the items an unemployed person who just lost their home and probably obtained significant debt weren't buying.

Scott never thought about this. Most people think he shouldn't have invested primarily in manufacturing but his industry showed not to be the issue.

When looking at new companies, his considerations swayed towards where margins were high and he could create opportunities to expand their client reach. If he invested in companies focused on manufacturing basic consumer household goods, cosmetics, or snacks, his portfolio would have balanced.

Do not feel bad for Scott. His portfolio bounced back. Some companies survived and he helped create a business continuity plan for future recessions.

Startup investing is tough. There are a lot of unknowns as well a lot of areas to think about. There is no algorithm available to invest blindly and expect success every time. Even with proper due diligence, you cannot expect success every time. These people are savvy investors, yet they make mistakes too. Learn from their mistakes so you do not make them.

Chapter Five : Choosing the Right Investor

A tug of war ensues once the founder has completed their pitch. The founder possesses the advantage at first and then the investor pulls the rope by counter offering and asking questions.

Founders must do their due diligence on an investor because all investors are not the same. Review the qualities an ideal investor holds in Chapter 3. Which ones do you agree with as a founder and why is it important to you they hold those qualities or characteristics? Go beyond agreeing with the qualities written in this book. Decide your own values and qualifications of what the right investor looks like to you.

Story: Choosing the Wrong Investor

A few years ago, I taught a small group of entrepreneurs and creatives about operating in a lean-agile way. An entrepreneur in my network started an organization for local creatives who were starting their own business. One of the attendees and I held a lengthy conversation. I will call her Veronica. She thrived in the education space like me and organized a lot of work to seek funding. Though she tried out for *Shark Tank* (and made it), she decided not to go this route and found other investors.

Her product sparked interest from many people, including me. At the time I wasn't investing and if I were, they were too far along in the startup stage for me. She developed a flagship product and companies issued letters of intent showing readiness to stock a certain quantity of goods in their stores. Unfortunately, she could not fulfill orders because like many entrepreneurs, she stood as a one-woman band.

Veronica found an angel investor willing to give more capital but for the opportunity to own 50% of her startup. She thought they would make an exceptional team. By this time, she became tired of the many pitches and low valuations. She felt she didn't have any other choice if she was going to fulfill the orders coming at her.

After a month, her investor's attitude changed. The investor originally stated he would provide her free rein to own and operate the business while he would stay a silent investor. I'm not sure if he invested in other companies, but he seemed to lack experience. Veronica completed no due diligence on him and his experience, and he did little diligence on her and her company. "He just seemed like a likeable person," she explained to me several times during our conversation.

She found out the investor's wife wanted involvement and sensed a huge upside potential in the product Veronica and her husband owned. Through her husband, the wife found a prime opportunity to use him to influence the direction of the company. Though he did not feel the same way as his wife, he continued to drive her agenda. This caused a huge lull in the progression of the company and their relationship. Veronica was eventually able to dissolve the agreement and go back on her own.

Though this guy may have been a great investor for her, he up ended being the wrong one for the direction she was taking the business. A properly written agreement between the two could have stopped the intervention of the investor's wife; and Veronica would have kept succeeding with the path she was going. It was a big lesson learned for her but to-date, she has decided not to take any further investment.

Trends in Angel Investing

Angel Investors traditionally provide funding for early stage startups. The increased interest in startup investing has made way for more investors to come into the fold, however it has not increased the investment power to early stage startups. This rise in investors pivoted the focus of high risk, high reward, early stage startups to lesser risk, more predictable reward from more established startups.

According to the UNH Center of Research[5], seed stage startup investing has decreased, and early stage startup investing has stayed the same. There is an increase in funding when the company is looking to expand, because investors see the growth. This removes some risk related to the seed stage startup with only a "good idea." I foresee the pool of seed-stage investors becoming smaller, with more investors waiting to invest in startups with traction. It's all about their investment model and where they choose to inject their capital.

Corporations can also be angel investors though they are many times overlooked as a source of funding. More corporations are looking at startup investing to stimulate the economy and help diversify their portfolio. Larger businesses possess a unique set of skills any founder must consider. With the level of influence and experience a Fortune 500 can have on your startup, you could definitely increase your chances of building a successful company.

Larger companies invest in startups intending to help them build and grow. Startups provide over a 2.5 million jobs each year to the U.S. economy. Corporations realize this and elect being part of this growing number. If you look at the mission and vision statements of most Fortune 500 companies, in some form they include value, quality, being a leader, and innovation into their statements. Your startup isn't large yet, but you want those same values in your company. Why? Corporations are more likely to invest in startups with similar values.

Corporations who invest also have an extensive network of people on their side. They have some of the best talent in operations, technology, finance, etc. People you could use to gain momentum where your company has gaps. Large corporations also have a portfolio of small, medium, and large businesses they work with. Financial services companies such as Bank of America work to bring their portfolio of clients together in a way to increase the profits of every size business they work with. Someone told me a Fortune 500 company, if they wanted to, could turn a startup into a multimillion-dollar business in the course of only a few short months. What a powerful statement. And after working for many large companies, I can see why. The power of the people and businesses they can connect a founder with is unbelievable!

Due Diligence on the Investor

An important part of due diligence for the founder is executing diligence on the investor and their firm. Choosing investors who are providing more than just money is a must when you start your Series A round and beyond. Save the money-only investors for your friends and family round or when your company is running like a well oiled machine and only needs capital to continue. Investors who only offer money and are not willing to put in sweat equity may not see your vision and possibly only see you as a source of income or tax write-off at the end of the year. Also, investors don't just invest in companies and industries they're familiar with anymore. In the early years of startup investing, investors only injected capital into industries and companies they were familiar with. It's not the case in today's investment world. This means founders do not always need to require an investor to come from an obvious place. Investors are now small business owners, retirees, college professors, and even your neighbors. When you talk to people, always keep pitching in mind. You never know if the guy you meet in your local grocery store possesses startup capital, business connections, knowledge, and likes your idea.

I challenge you, the founder, to make a list of investors you want to approach based on doing due diligence on them first. Now is the time. Let's do it!

Questions to Investors

A founder must have some expectations for their investor. There are questions you can ask an investor like "What characteristics do you have that will make you a good investor for me?" First ask yourself the challenging question, "What characteristics do I have to make me a good founder?" It is essential to create your own standards if you will expect to question an investor about their abilities and experience.

What are some characteristics you want to see in a founder?

Look introspectively. If you do not have the characteristics an investor likes, you two MAY NOT have a compatible relationship. This is a working relationship like you would have with a co-founder. Even if you don't possess all the characteristics, it doesn't mean your partnership will not be great. Identify your core qualities!

What multiple of investment returns are you looking for?

This sets an expectation for the investors. As a founder, you probably have your own financial goals for at least the next three years.

If you formally pitched your business, you came in with an idea of what kind of return you expect to provide. If you cannot meet these expectations, you can have a conversation with the investor to re-evaluate financial expectation before moving forward.

What type of companies do you invest in?
Alternate Question: What deals have you already done?
This reveals a lot about an investor. Do they only invest in companies in their wheelhouse of knowledge? For experienced investors with a larger portfolio, this is not always the case. If you are not in any industries or have any synergies with the other companies in your investor's portfolio, likely you're a project for your investor. This could be risky for you, so understand why they are interested in your company. Receiving a barrage of simple questions related to your industry means your investor most likely has not invested in a company like yours.

Do you have references of companies you worked with?
Investors may call on your customers and employees. Conversely, you may call on current and past founders they have relationships with. There are some simple questions you can ask other founders to help you get a sense of how the investor operates.

- What type of relationship do you have with the investor?
- What are some of his/her pet peeves as it relates to business?
- What type of value does the investor brought to your companies?
- What do you feel like the investor is missing that you wish they had?
- Did the investor ever provide additional funding when you needed it?

Founders will openly provide you feedback on the expectations of the investor, how to work with them, and habits to avoid when dealing with the investor. They could save you a lot of time and headache.

Do you have a website/online presence?

Some investment companies are very private and may not have an online presence. Venture Capital firms have a better online presence. Since they work with the capital of many people and organizations, their online presence is simpler to locate. Even if they do not have a website, most investment firms have an online profile created as a registered investment firm.

What are your expectations of me and the company?

Be open and honest with your investor. Make sure both of you relay the expectations of working together as a team. Many times an investor will present you with boiler plate responses like, "come in early and work late," "be transparent," "execute effectively," "interact with your customers," or my favorite, "be willing to break the rules and think outside of the box." Investors provide this feedback but it's not until you work with them when you realize their true expectations. They won't tell you they're indecisive, not business savvy, or uncommitted to fresh ideas. This is why reaching out to the investor's current or previous founders will help ensure a successful relationship.

What's your long-term vision for the company?

Strategic investors think about the long-term play on your business the moment you finish your pitch. Good business-minded investors invest for the long-term growth, not so much the short-term returns. If they have a large portfolio, they may have realized synergies in their other business which could help build traction (or more traction). They may have people in their network who will take your business to the next level. Now they're not going to always see the synergies immediately, but most investors stay well connected and understand the benefits of having a significant network.

Do you have a team? If so, what are their skills?

It's important investors bring something to the table other than capital when you're at the earliest stages. A network is important, but also having an excellent team is a great bonus. My investment group has a team with sales and marketing people, finance gurus, lawyers, doctors, and even IT professionals. We share an entrepreneurial spirit and use our skills to help our companies. Finding an investor with a solid team will benefit you.

Are you an active or passive investor?

There's no wrong answer here. It depends on your preference. Active investors are important, especially at the seed stage. You want them to invest sweat equity to help your business grow. Sweat equity doesn't mean they'll be working in your company every day, but they will work with you in an advisory role and/or providing you with the right visibility to gain more funding. Most investors will not have time to sit by your side on a day-to-day basis, but they need to bring additional value to the table other than a check.

If you feel you have enough investors providing sweat equity to help your company grow, this is the time to consider cash-only investors. Cash with no support could be detrimental to the future success of your startup so make strategic decisions on who you have investing in your company from the start.

Do you have a success story from one or more of your investment companies?

If you're asking this question, you want to know if their contributions are leading to growth, IPOs, buyouts, etc. Investors also quantify their success by "successful exits" when they have profited and given back their equity to the company. It's not enough to have money, a network, and a team if none of them lead to results. Your startup needs to deliver results. Your investor, if they have a good portfolio, must produce results.

When you invest, how will you distribute money?

Once an investor pumps capital into your business, they will not always deliver the entire amount you requested. Spain-based angel investing crowdfunding platform, Startupxplore, lays out a nice structure on who, what, when, and how they invest in companies. Not all investors will or can tell you this upfront. They wait until the term sheet or final agreement to expose the expected payment method. This will depend on the investor's operating model or what they find during due diligence signaling when you need more funding.

How much do you normally invest in a company?

I sometimes discuss this in the first meeting. Through some research, it may be easy to find out this information before pitching. If you're in a one-on-one pitch with an investor, they may provide you with their own introduction including the range of dollars they inject into a business. When working with angel syndicates, their investment range may vary but you can find them on their website.

Have you ever needed to inject more money into a company?

This is a mindset question. It's important to know if your investor is ready and willing to invest additional capital, if needed, into your business. Since your company has not started making a profit, it's important to have investors who are ready and willing to inject more capital into your business without going through the hassle of looking for new investors.

Are you willing to lead the round?

The investor who leads the round drives the investment round. By leading a round, an investor agrees to put the greatest, and sometimes first, capital injection into your startup. You'll very seldom hear about a single angel investor leading a round. It's often an investment group, syndicate or VC firm. Those who lead the round bring in more investors they know to invest in your startup. Before you know it, the round will be closed.

The Life of a Fund-Seeking Founder

Raising capital is a second job for a founder. On top of the chaos you deal within your startup, you must keep up with the changes in your industry and find new potential investors. As a founder looking for serious rounds of capital, you will spend sixty percent or more of your time looking for funding and pitching your business. If you are a solo entrepreneur with a small team or no team, learn to manage your time wisely.

In an interview with Auxbus Founder, Dan Radin, he stated the best and first piece of advice a friend ever gave him comprised of keeping his cash burn rate low. At the time his first funding round started, his burn rate already averaged $10,000. As he continued to grow his team, it quickly grew from $10,000 to $20,000, then $30,000. Auxbus, a startup based out of Asheville, North Carolina showed much promise but experienced a tough time acquiring capital. When they finally received an injection, they burned through it in almost nine months. I believe part of their downfall included their focus of looking only at angel capital locally. Don't let the pool of local investors discourage you, there are options to reach investors from anywhere. They could have received a spread of capital across geographic locations. Dan knew how much of a burden this would be on his business.

He stated you can't spend 60-90% of your time not developing your business and looking for funding. It's a frustrating process and with the amount of early stage investors slowly decreasing, the pool of investors become more difficult to find. With his business burning money at twenty to thirty thousand dollars a month, it wasn't worth his time to wait months on an investor who commit to writing a check of five to twenty thousand dollars. This became even more frustrating when an investor backed out after three months of diligence.

It's very important to understand the deal flow of syndicates and VCs. Deal flow shows the process and rate in which an investment firm can intake new startups and provide them capital. Most experienced firms have this in place. Well-known investors can receive dozens of business plans and proposals to pitch every month. They must create an efficient funnel to find the one company to invest in. Don't think the job of an investor is easy. They must have a good vetting process and criteria to keep the backlog of potential founders moving before they lose out on their unicorn.

Founders, you must have the skill of discerning initial advice for an offer of mentorship. There are investors out there who will treat you like a person and not just an investment. Investors will give you guidance on your company even before they invest. This doesn't mean they automatically become your mentor. After they say "no", I will not invest, you can burn a bridge by sending constant follow-up emails month after month in hopes of more advice. Most will provide you advice at the moment with the expectation to never hear from you again. There are investors who will request you stay in contact with them so they can track your progress. Then there are the mighty few who will volunteer to mentor you and help your business. If you're a fan of *Shark Tank*, you may remember Daymond John offering to mentor twelve-year-old Mo Bridges who owned the company Mo's Bows. For busy investors, this seldom happens but enjoy the opportunity if you receive it. The investor will direct how they would like to proceed with you. Don't force a connection that did not exist.

Chapter Six: Diligence

Delivering Diligence

At the writing of this book, there's no television show covering what due diligence entails. Even in *Beyond the Tank*, there's no discussion around due diligence findings or why a Shark didn't end up investing. Why? Because due diligence isn't sexy, and it's not the happiest part of entrepreneurship for the investor or the entrepreneur. For the entrepreneur, it is the most stressful.

From the perspective of an investor, due diligence reveals pertinent information about the founder and how they run their business. Investors don't expect everything to be perfect in the business, however they possess a list of standards the business and founder must maintain. They realize it's a startup and there will be room for improvement.

Often, investors begin the due diligence process and what the founder originally presented don't match what the company stated during the pitch. Financials is a very common number to get wrong or embellish upon. I don't mean the numbers were off by an insignificant amount, but by tens of thousands of dollars. Investors want to make sure the business is worth the investment, but the founder and their business must put it all on the table to make it happen.

To invest in businesses during their seed stages is a blessing for me. Most startups own a minimum viable product (MVP) and are just pushing their product or service to market. I gather insights into what the customers are saying, issues they are having, and how it stacks up to other products or services they've used. This is where the real innovation begins. For me, due diligence really begins here. When I'm serious about working with a business, I want the relationship to go further by meeting the team and the customers. It's like a relationship when you meet your significant other's family. It's awkward in some ways. Most employees are friendly and not sure what to say. They know their gripes with the company could lead to a loss of funding for the company and a loss of their job. They also know if they're not truthful, the business will not receive the help it needs. Like in a relationship, you will find those team members who are the talkers and do not care if you're an investor or a bum off the street. If you have an ear to listen, they fill it with everything they can. Find those team members. They will be the greatest assets to your decision making.

As an angel, validation of customer discovery and customer insights of a seed stage startup is difficult. If the company has no customers, how do you properly know this is a product or service a customer needs or wants? Has the company chosen the right target customer? Is the idea good enough to meet the demands of multiple customer markets? It's hard to say, especially for companies like Uber who were major disrupters in the transportation industry. Therefore, you hear so many stories of investors regretting not investing in startups such as Ring, Uber, Apple, etc. Having domain knowledge or team members in the space is helpful. Otherwise, you rely on a series of gut feelings about the idea and the founder to make your decision.

Venture Capital Due Diligence

Many Venture Capitalists operate with a structured due diligence process. There's no industry standard. Based on your business, you can expect certain questions, and if the founder is in the pitching stage of their business, they've heard most of the questions. The second half of this book will cover many of those questions and why they make sense for an investor to ask and a founder to answer.

The Venture Capital world has a terrible reputation for investing in areas where no one has a domain knowledge. A VC can purchase a company, fire a bunch of employees to gain more profits for its investor pool. They will make a few process changes and close major deals to increase revenue, then sell before the company goes out of business. I agree this is poor practice and has caused more lawmakers to look at ways to regulate the VC and startup investment world.

The investment firm's sole priority is to produce returns for those who invest in their funds. To keep their reputation and investors happy, those returns are necessary by any means necessary. This is not what all VC firms do. It's the rotten apples who are spoiling the bunch. It really takes a firm to look at the long-term vision and support the vision to make companies great and profitable. Most companies increase their profits by just improving their internal processes and increasing their customer reach. Yes, a few jobs may be lost or repurposed but it should not be mass layoffs through the company. This refers to companies who have at least a hundred employees and are generating substantial revenue growth for their size. As a reminder, investors view and judge companies differently based on the stage in which their business is.

Due Diligence Process Steps

For those who are looking to invest with companies like mine, you can find my company's approach at www.afterthepitch.com/resources. If you're a new investor, this would be a brilliant starting point (pats self on back)!

After the pitch, the investor will email you contact information of the main due diligence contact and possibly all the members of the due diligence team. The point of contact (leader) will be your best friend for the next couple of weeks or months.

The leader will provide all the expectations of the due diligence process including the necessary paperwork, questions, and financials you must provide. Sometimes there's two leaders who are your points of contact in case industry knowledge does not translate well or as a backup. Translation issues could include one leader not possessing a certain knowledge of technology or the business aspects of the work being done by your company. Having another person on the team who can complement the other leader's knowledge helps the analysis process run smoothly.

Along with expectations, they will provide you the preferred methods of communication whether it be a standing daily call, an email, or text message. This process depends on the investor which is why it's so important founders own their internal processes of due diligence. It helps eliminate the heavy lifting upfront and allows the founders to continue pitching with no issues and their focus remains on gaining traction in their startup. Seasoned investors will provide communication tools or deal software to keep all information in the same place, making it easier for both you and them to collaborate.

The other scenario? You will hear nothing from the investor. If you do not hear from them, a courtesy call can help you gauge the interest of the investor. Just like in sales jobs, a founder figures out how many follow-up calls to make before realizing they can't gain ground with the investor. I call this your follow-up call ratio. Whether you call, email, or text, make sure you document your follow-ups. This is to figure out your follow-up call ratio. It's helpful when on the fifth call you get a response and the investor states they did not receive your messages. I hear the sweet spot is five follow-up calls before calling it quits.

How an Investor Views Due Diligence

Investors do not invest blindly into companies, at least most don't. They benchmark deals with other startups and find industry experts who can provide them insights into the legality of their investment's operating model. They understand their investment and the level of risk they're taking in providing capital to a business.

Due diligence is costly to an investor unless they have an effective process or team. There's no other way to say it other than you must have a documented and efficient process. Whether your process is thorough, it must be consistent each time. Initially, you will create a standard process then tweak it over time to accommodate lessons learned. The more tweaking you do, the more it will fit your needs and become your standard. Take an iterative approach to this process to figure out what works and what doesn't. It will take time. Possessing a process shows the investor holds a sense of urgency and professionalism to complete the deal. There's a lot on the line for an investor and the longer they wait to invest, the more the market and startup changes. The more you invest, you will realize time is money.

Building a team costs money too. Putting a proper team together is very important in making a sound investment decision. Not all investors have an investment team, but larger firms do. As a new investor, it's wise to have experts on your side who can fill some gaps in knowledge you do not possess. Lawyers and accountants are common professions you need to work with to close a deal. A legal and financial team can complete most of the due diligence for you, but it's costly. Investing with experienced investors, like I did, subsidizes the cost for these professionals. An investor should never ask a startup founder to foot the bill for any costs related to the due diligence process.

Many business lawyers are familiar with due diligence as they inherently complete due diligence on their clients. Though it's a unique process, it requires the same soft skills. Hiring the right lawyer is important. Not all lawyers are the same. Don't go hire your Uncle Joe who has been a divorce lawyer for 20 years. If your investment is real estate, you will want a real estate lawyer, if you're investing in a unique startup, you may want an Intellectual Property lawyer amongst other types of lawyers. Even though you do not know the law, it's important for you to know what type of legal services you need.

There are benefits to being the first investor to go through due diligence. You first drive the value of the business. Numbers are more negotiable when a founder has no other investment outside of FFF. You can likely receive a larger equity percentage or create opportunities for yourself no other investor will receive. On the flip side of this, you've done all the legwork for another investor to come in, use your analysis, and make an investment consuming less time and money. It doesn't matter because if you invest, this may influence others to as well.

How a Founder Views Due Diligence

The earlier the stage, the less information you possess to present an investor. Do not worry about it, present what you have. Assume you're at least a year into the startup. You've created this idea, developed an MVP, and went through a detailed level of customer discovery. It's reasonable this has all taken a year's time. Now you understand the validity of your startup and you consider pitching to investors. You've perfected your pitch and now have an investor on the hook. How do you think of the next steps?

First, a founder must choose an investor as much as an investor has to choose a founder and its company. Chapter 5 covers this thoroughly. To say this decision is one-sided is not true. Don't be afraid to decline a deal with an Investor who doesn't fit you. It's easy to focus on the money instead of the actual value of the investor. Novice founders can make colossal mistakes in their first round of investing. They could choose investors who want to steal the company from under them. This happens when founders grant too much equity without considering the true value the investor brings to the table. Yes, money is value but sweat equity, knowledge, and connections are too. If an investor is leading a round, will they work to bring you more investors or just take a sizable piece of the pie and tell you how to run your business.

What type of investor are you looking for? Do they have industry knowledge? Do they have an extensive network? Are they a leader in the industry who can provide expert knowledge to enhance what you do and provide mentorship? Only you as a founder know what you need in an investor other than an investment. If it's not already in the agreement, they expect to gain a seat on your board of directors. Capital is not the only asset your company needs. If an investor buys into your business at this stage, they need to come to the table with more.

In early stage startups, founders need to take an inventory of sweat equity put forward to keep their business running. Often there are several founders doing all the work. They'll split their percentage stake in the company. Their work to build the business creates value. Actually, this provides major value when you're not paying employees and consultants to build the business. During due diligence, sweat equity creates new value.

If you acquire "money only" investors in your portfolio, but they shouldn't make up the majority. You want your investor to fall into one or more of these categories.

1. Industry Leader
2. Long-Term Investor

3. Growth Investor

Making it to a completed deal is almost poetic. It's a dance between the investor and the founder. There's much uniqueness in the process because every investor and founder are different. It doesn't matter who leads, but through the process, your steps will naturally flow into one another. That's why I'm providing you with this information.

For the savvy syndicates and VCs, they take a lot of the work out of your hands and lead the diligence process. They'll ask you for access to documentation and tools, and they will do the rest. The impressive part about this is they will craft a story for you of your business you can use with other investors

Creating the Plan

The process starts with the investor. First, individual angel investors will complete the due diligence process by themselves or with fellow angels if it's a syndicate. Venture Capitalist will have a due diligence team with a primary leader, or there may be a group of venture capitalist and/or angels who make up the due diligence team. It will be the lead investor who will do most of the work during the due diligence process and report back to the team. The more established a firm, the more structured the process will be. An alternative option is having the investment firm outsource some or all the due diligence process to a third party.

Minimum requirements for due diligence teams include:
- A list of key answers important to the investor
- Company bylaws
- Executive Team Summary
- List of suppliers, vendors, and board members

- Business Plan or Business Model Canvas (depending on investor's preference)
- Financials which can include a plethora of models, the financial structure and financing history of the company
- Operations Summary
- Technology stack used to operate the business
- Intellectual property (including all patent, copyright, and trademark information)

Your business plan establishes a list of key answers important to investors however you can also provide the investor with an FAQ from the start. The business plan provides a thorough analysis into your startup and how it operates. An important part of the business plan is the financial forecasting. I would encourage you to add this as a benchmark for the investor to look over.

Some founders create their business model canvas and provide a summary of each area. For your own business model canvas template, visit www.afterthepitch.com/resources. This will mimic your pitch. You lead with the problem you're looking to solve and who you're looking to solve it for (customer segment). State your solution (value proposition) once this is pronounced. Once there is a good understanding of your business, the best sections to include is how you plan to reach, obtain, and build your customer portfolio. Who are key partners who can help you get to your goals? The key activities and employees (key resources) are important to understanding how the company will operate and grow. Finally, what your revenue model looks like in a summary. There's no need to go into your detailed costs for forecasts when creating a business model canvas. Save those details for the Financials section in your business plan.

Your company bylaws and operating agreement(s) are very important to establishing a company structure. They are working documents, meaning you will continuously update them. As you add investors, your bylaws will require updating too.

After the due diligence process, the founder receives a proposed term sheet which includes the terms and conditions of the investment relationship and a confirmation or revision to the valuation of the company. If you've raised money previously, provide the potential investor with due diligence reports from past investors or potential investors who went through the process but did not invest.

Most due diligence is virtual, however plan for a site visit or two during the process. Even if you're running the business out of your garage, home office, or a co-working space. Investors sometimes want a walk-through of your operations.

Communication Planning

When going through the diligence process, investors and their teams want to speak with other individuals than just the founder. Everyone associated with your company is fair game. Personally, I like to speak to close advisors, employees, and clients. Sometimes I've even spoken to clients' employees. Those are the individuals who don't have an invested stake in the startup either way but use their product or service. They provide the most direct feedback and they're not scared of the owner of the company. There are reasons investors target specific groups. Important startup information comes from different avenues, not just from the financials. Communication is completed methodically and can include working with:

- Founders
- Employees
- Investors who have injected capital
- Advisors

- Board of Directors
- Clients

If employees in the company exist, it's very important to have communications with the team members. These one-on-one conversations help you understand the structure of the team. It's also a splendid time to understand the culture of the team. Most individuals perceive an investor as someone who plans to come into the company and help it grow, which will relieve the employees of their frustrations. Make it a good idea to speak with them. By working in a volatile environment, they're likely working because they believe in the company and want to watch it succeed. Unlike larger companies, employees often work despite hating the job. Startup employees have different perspective being in on the ground floor of a new company.

Once you meet with the team members, you will have the right ammunition to speak with everyone else on the list. You'll understand the startup's culture, structure, processes, and the overall strengths, weaknesses, and opportunities. You'll learn more about threats through industry knowledge and clients than from the team members.

Speaking with other investors, if the company has any, is the litmus test I use before moving forward to the official due diligence process. Communicating with fellow investors who have already provided capital compares to sitting around in a barbershop or salon all day. You'll hear all the gossip and get all the information you need from an investment standpoint. Investors are open to speaking with another investor freely. This will leave you understanding how to best work with the founder and what pain points or gaps need work.

Besides co-founders, the founder's advisors are the ones who show their support in the most intimate ways. Advisors hold the most influence over the founder's decisions in business. They're also the founder's confidants when things go wrong, and they need to vent. These individuals are not always savvy business professionals. Advisors can be friends, relatives, and school professors who have been sounding boards and stepped into an advisory role for the founder. Communicating with the advisors and mentors is a superb way to understand how the founder's mind works. It's also great when the founder is receiving the right guidance. Advice from individuals who don't run a successful business or knows little about business can be detrimental.

Like advisors and mentors, the company's board of directors hold the influence. Professionals who know either the industry or know about business need to make up the board. The makeup of a board should also be diverse. I've known boards to possess lawyers, accountant, business executives, business consultants, other startup founders, and industry influencers. Once a startup asks for funds, I'm always curious as to the amount each board member has contributed financially to the business. It's important for me to know the members on the board invest financially. If they're not able to contribute money, maybe they're only looking to reap benefits of its success. I met a founder who developed an amazing board of directors. None however injected capital into the business. The key members of the board comprised well known community leaders. One worked with high net-worth athletes and business owners however never introduced the founder to any of his connections. What does it say about the board members? Do they not believe in the founder? Is the company too risky to invest in?

Investor-Customer Interviews

It's the founder's job to provide a list of clients and communicate to the client the who, what, and why of receiving a request for an investor interview. To be clear, make sure the client is the user and benefactor of the product or service provided by the startup. You could get a list of business owners who never used a product, but their employees have. In this case, the investors want to speak to the employees. Speaking with the employees who use the product or service will provide them two key components; what's wrong with the product or service, and how has the startup interacted with the employee to make sure their concerns were being addressed properly. That's all they need to know from the company's clients. If there are varying customer segments, say a business and an individual consumer, the investor will interview the different customer segments.

Validation

The due diligence report (also known as a due diligence disclosure packet) includes the assessment and validation of market, financials, legal structure, tax documentation, and company projections. As a founder, it is wise to ask for the final report, however some investors will not provide it. It's a thorough assessment from the experienced professionals on where you need to focus and enhance your business. This is a noble way to get an external unbiased view of where your startup stands. For an established startup with at least five years in business, your report may include much of the following.

Summary of Corporate Records
- State of incorporation and standings with the state
- Issued shares of stock
- Articles of Incorporation and bylaws
- List of shareholders
- Copies of all correspondence with shareholders
- Existence of any warrants, options, or other potential equity

Summary of Financial Information
- Copies of audited financial statements for the past five years
- Copies of correspondence between management and auditors
- List of federal and state jurisdictions where the seller has filed taxes for the past five years
- Federal, state, and local tax returns for the past five years
- All boards of directors' presentations and meeting minutes
- All financial models and forecasts

Summary of Liability/Debt
- Investigate debts of startup
- Loan Agreements
- Mortgages
- Equity Agreements
- Convertible Notes
- Review correspondence with lenders

Validation of Employment and Labor
- List and biographies of officers, board of directors, and employees
- List of employees, background checks, their job function, department, location and compensation
- Agreement of employee profit sharing, deferred compensation, equity, and other non-salary compensation or benefits
- Copies of employee handbook
- Important findings from employee interviews
- Copies of employment, consulting, termination, parachute and indemnity agreements
- Pending litigation related to labor and employment law

Validation & Summary of Real Estate
- Real estate lease agreements

- Address and legal description for all properties
- Copies of titles
- Copies of real estate appraisals
- Copies of site evaluations and reports

Summary of Agreements
- Agreements entered by the company
- Partnership, joint venture, and/or operating agreements
- Marketing, sales, and distributor agreements
- Broker or investment banker agreements
- Client/customer agreements
- Licenses
- Subscriptions

Supplier and Customer Information
- List of all material customers including dollar amounts and volume of sales
- Results from reference calls/interviews
- List of all material suppliers including dollar and volume of purchases
- Correspondence with customers or suppliers related to complaints or disputes

Summary of Legal Documents
- Copies of each report or document filed with government agencies
- Descriptions of all litigation, administrative proceeding, governmental investigations
- Copies of all government licenses
- Environmental liability assessments and environmental compliance audits

Overall Assessment
- Summation of important findings from the above category
- SWOT Analysis based on industry, market reach, company findings, and financials
- Recommended Valuation

Most investors will scroll down to the "overall assessment" section, then review other sections based on the findings of the due diligence team. A thorough due diligence team takes all the guesswork out of company evaluations. Remember, you will pay for the convenience.

Negotiation and Injection

Once the investor completes due diligence and they present the final report, everything revolves around valuation. Everyone understands the valuation created by the founder, and the investor will or will not validate it at this point. The founder and investor now conclude of what additional value the investor has to offer. There will be some non-negotiables both parties have determined. Before due diligence starts, both parties should know what they're not willing to offer or hand over. An investor may want an additional five percent equity for the perceived value they bring. For the founder, is it too much to hand over five percent?

A founder also has to consider what kind of equity shares to provide the investor. There are two types; common stock and preferred stock. Usually common stock is issued early in the funding stages. Owners of common stock are the last to receive profits in order of debt importance. Experienced investors will often request preferred stock which can also be converted into common shares at a later point. The benefits of preferred shares versus common are these stocks allow the investor to be paid sooner in the event of a merger, acquisition, or IPO. Preferred shares however have no voting rights when it comes to the startup, their policies, or electing board of directors.

If the founder has already raised money, they have other investors to consider. If you are handing over more equity, it may negatively affect the equity of other investors. This is when dilution happens. First, have a conversation with your current investors and find out if they're willing to dilute their stake in the startup. If they understand how the new investor can grow the company (outside of providing money), they are more amenable to the dilution, because it could help the startup grow faster.

Example of Dilution

If Investor A owns 20% of a startup valued at $1 million, their stake is worth $200,000. The founder then goes into a new round of investing and the valuation becomes $2 million. Investor B leads the round by injecting $2 million at a $3 million pre-revenue valuation. The new value of the company becomes $5 million ($2 million plus $3 million). Investor A then gets diluted by 40% ($2 million divided by $5 million). Now investor A owns 12% (20% minus (20% times 40%)) of the startup. The 12% is now worth $600,000 (12% times $5 million) with a gain of $400,000.

The benefit to the current investor is when the valuation increases, or the new investor brings in so much value it increases profits significantly. It's possible to negotiate dilution within your term sheet.

Term Sheet

Your term sheet must describe what happens upon the founders exiting the company. This is important to the investor more than the founder. What does the investor's payout look like? Will they have a limited stake in the company? If a limited stake, what are the contingencies of a buyout. Here, contingencies complicate a deal and the founder should avoid this in any agreement.

Finally, with the term sheet completed and signed, you will receive your funds. There are two primary ways to transfer funds. The investor transfers the funds via an escrow account. The investor opens their own account, or the escrow account belongs to a third party. The investor puts the funds in the escrow account at the end of due diligence with the expectations of investing. There may be criteria or milestones the founder must reach for increments or all the money to be distributed for the startup. The investor holds the funds there for safe-keeping until the founder meets all the conditions set.

The investor will also wait for the founder to complete the conditions and send a direct transfer from bank to bank. It is a simple process however, there's been situations where the bank makes errors. In an episode of Startup Podcast with Chris Sacca, his bank fat fingered a number on Gimlet Media's bank account number. The wire went to another bank account, and the owner of the account immediately withdrew most of the money. Hopefully, this will never happen to you.

The completion of your first term sheet is a huge milestone. Closing out your first round is an even bigger milestone. Congratulations on making it this far. Take the time to celebrate this accomplishment, whether you're an investor or founder. It only gets better from here.

Chapter Seven: Beyond Due Diligence

Oversight

A sign of maturity for a founder is having a board of directors providing oversight and guidance on how the company is run. There's major skepticism and misconceptions with creating a board of directors for your business. The doubt comes from popular stories of CEOs being ousted from their own companies by their board. The option of choosing a board of directors over advisors is control. Advisors do exactly what their title implies, advise. You can count on them as your sounding board or your support when you're struggling. Most advisors possess a particular skill set or expertise in a specific area of business. The advisor's job is to improve the way you do business, gain traction, and grow your business. Advisors believe in you as a founder and do what they can to support you.

The board of directors provide similar guidance and advice, the key difference is the board of directors operates based on the corporation's bylaws. They are also a group who works in the best interest of the company to resolve issues, conflicts, and holds the CEO accountable to a strategic plan needed to make the company successful. At the earlier stages, your board contains investors, businesspeople, and entrepreneurs, who own specific expertise needed and possess the network of individuals to support the CEO's vision. At later stages, the company's shareholders elect a board of directors to drive business growth. Lets go back though. Why would a founder get ousted from their own company?

Being Ousted

Jack Ma (Alibaba), Steph Korey (Away), Brad Dickerson (Blue Apron), Kevin Plank (Under Armour), Adam Neuman (WeWork), and others are all founders who became ousted or "stepped down" from their roles as CEO of their companies. Stepping down typically means the board of directors gave the CEO an option to either be fired or step down from their position. It happens not only with startups but Fortune 500 companies.

Founders become weary of a board of directors when they consider companies such as Apple. The board removed Steve Jobs from his role in the company. This is probably the most infamous story of a CEO in technology history. At thirty years of age, they removed Steve Jobs from the life and legacy he built over the previous nine years. He changed the way the world viewed technology.

For those who have not heard or read about Steve Jobs, friends who knew him touted him as a creative perfectionist. Though he inspired innovation, he also expected excellence from those who worked for him. Some of his employees would compare working with him to working at a "sweat shop." This was not the entire issue with the board of directors.

Jobs voluntarily stepped down from the role as CEO to lead the division of Macintosh (now called Mac). As his replacement, he hired the head of Pepsi-Cola, John Sculley. This move, being consensual and strategic for Jobs, meant he would work on his Mac vision. With Sculley's experience, he displayed a natural fit and their relationship began great.

The Macintosh division became its own separate entity. It possessed its own building and housed its own employees. Of all divisions of Apple, the Macintosh group bled the most money. Employees complained about Jobs and said he was unbearable to work with. This put the nail in his coffin. As Sculley worked to remediate the issues, the relationship between the two became crushing. Sculley, unable to handle the strong opinions of Steve Jobs, took his concerns to the board. They agreed to relocate Jobs. He lost his office, and the board placed him in oppressive work conditions. This forced him to leave his own company, eventually.

Though he left his company and went into depression, Steve Jobs succeeded and returned to the company. At Job's 2005 Stanford commencement address, he stated being fired from Apple let him "enter one of the most creative periods" in his life. During this time Steve Jobs possessed the mental space to fall in love with Laurene Powell, his wife. The situation with Jobs, though it felt detrimental to his life, ended up creating more abundance mentally. He just didn't realize it then. As he stated in his speech about love and loss, "You can't connect the dots looking forward, you can only connect the dots looking backwards." He never imagined what being away from Apple would do for him. He ended up creating Pixar and a computer and software company called NeXT. Disney and Apple acquired each, respectively.

In the words of Steve Jobs, "How can you get fired from a company you started?" If you're a corporation, it's easy as a CEO of a startup with a board of investors, you're only part owner of the company. The structure of a board of directors dictates their obligation (and the founders) to create an extensive set of bylaws and expectations for each executive position. If you do not abide by the bylaws or expectations, the board possesses the right to vote and fire you. Remember, the board is working in the best interest of the company, not the founder. Based on the bylaws and the job expectations set upon the CEO, the board didn't fail the company, the CEO failed the company. Something similar happened with Elon Musk, however he made the choice to step down as Chairman of the board for the "interest of the company" though he remained CEO.

The fear of losing control is only due to having a board. The fear lies in the company possessing more structure than an agile, ever-changing startup. Founders need to be adaptable in becoming structured with a level of standards. There's no transition coaching for founders who formerly worked in the startup world and they have troubles adjusting to a structured corporation. Some do well while others don't. The founder who developed the original culture must endure company culture change just as much as its employees must adapt to the change.

With growth of your company, it is still in your best interest to have a board of directors. They will allow you to grow and become established enough to take your company public if your goal for growth includes going public. Major sponsors and investors view a board of directors as a non-negotiable part of partnering with a company. Taking your company to the next level is important and the best way to do it is with a board of directors.

The Exit Strategy

Exiting a startup is stressful for you, the founder. You've spent time and money into "your baby" and now you must grasp not being able to call the shots, work with the team you created, and grow it to the vision you perceive for the company. It's natural for you to get cold feet about exiting. What will you do next? Is there another idea you're passionate about?

Exits are natural parts of the process for both founders and investors. There are five unique types of exits to consider; the Initial Public

Offering (IPO), the acquisition, the sell/buyout, recapitalization, or the liquidation of the business.

Private and Public Ownership

There are two fundamental types of company ownership, private and public ownership. There's a small majority of dual-class companies, such as Ford and Berkshire Hathaway, who are both publicly and privately owned. Privately owned (also privately traded or privately held) companies are predominantly owned by the founder of the company. There may be family members or investors as part owners, however the founder is likely the main owner. Think of your local food truck or mom and pop restaurant. Privately owned companies make up most companies in the world. With privately traded companies, investors cannot gain an ownership stake in the company through the stock market. The only way they can receive equity interest is by contacting the owner directly.

There are approximately 630,000 companies publicly traded all over the world. In the United States, however, there's approximately 3,000 publicly traded companies. This is the dream for a founder to reach the Initial Public Offering (IPO) stage. The IPO is where most founders strive to be because it demonstrates their startup is a legit company. There's a long and costly process involved in preparing your company to get listed on the stock exchange. There's a load of paperwork and due diligence. Additionally, founders have to reach many big investors to persuade them there's value in bringing the company to Wall Street. This is months of work and traveling to meet with investors and show them the value and strength of your business.

To grow your company to a point when you're invited to ring the starting bell on the New York Stock Exchange (NYSE) is unbelievable. Few startup founders ever receive the opportunity. Traditionally, it is the best way to increase your reach to obtain additional funding. Today there are major declines in publicly traded companies. In just the last ten years, the number of publicly traded companies has declined by over fifty percent.

IPO or No?

There are several speculations on why companies are not choosing to go public. The first are the ever changing and sometimes ignorant regulations the government puts in place to control publicly traded companies. I do not believe their intentions are malicious; they want to make sure the U.S. economy stays in the black. On the opposite side of the coin, the federal government has deterred companies to go public. The stress of paperwork and costs alone is enough to drive a founder mad.

Remember the 2008 economic crash? This devastated many households who placed their trust in Wall Street. The crash helped consumers and investors learn about optional ways to invest their money and not keep it tied to the stock market. This made a way for more private investing.

Technology increases a company's reach to investors all over the globe. The entire purpose of companies going public is to increase their funding for future growth and capital expenses. The internet alone allows business to increase their reach through online platforms without the need to go public. If a founder can maintain broader, less risky options, shouldn't they consider them? These less risky options are more appetizing for small capitalization (cap) companies. Those are business who possess a total stock value or smaller market capitalization. Ten years ago, those companies made up a large percentage of the stock market, though they only held

$300 million to $2 billion in market cap. Now, these companies find private funding options more beneficial, less timely, and not as costly.

Luckily, our economy hasn't crashed, but for a simple reason. The stock market doesn't thrive from the quantity of companies on the exchange, it thrives from the collective monetary value of the companies. Over time, these publicly traded companies continue to increase their value. They too benefit from technology, but in a different way. Technology growth and acquisitions of other publicly and privately traded companies brings more value to larger companies. The increased value of the few thousand companies offsets the loss of over seven thousand small cap companies. This shouldn't discourage any company from the IPO process. Now there are options other than the "traditional way."

The IPO is the most talked about exit strategy in the technology startup world. Going public is profitable for the founder and investors. It's a quick way to make millionaires or billionaires out of young founders who created a business from their garage, dorm, or a co-working space.

Acquisition

Being acquired by a company or individual is a less stressful option. Since you've been through the pitch processes and due diligence, you'll be doing the same activities. Acquisitions can come from individuals, VC, or other companies. You often hear the words "merger" and "acquisition" mentioned synonymously however they have two different meanings. In a merger, two companies have synergies with one another, and they come together to form a new company. Consider BB&T and SunTrust Banks coming together to form Truist Bank. The two companies believed the merger would help their growth strategy, so they joined forces. In 1998, Exxon

Corporation and Mobil Corporation not only merged companies but their name became ExxonMobil. It's still known as one of the largest mergers in U.S. history. Sirius and XM Radio did the same ten years later with what is now SiriusXM. They also acquired Pandora in 2018 but kept the Pandora brand.

Larger companies may acquire a smaller one without merging. The larger company or the company with the best brand recognition keeps their name in these cases. When Sprint acquired Nextel, kept Sprint's name. The only remnants of Nextel was their colors black and yellow. WeWork acquired Naked Hub in 2015 to expedite its expansion of co-working locations but left the Naked Hub name behind.

Sometimes in acquisition, the dominant company discerns there is more benefit in keeping the companies separate, or at least their brands separate, and operating in a joint venture type of way. Financially, brand recognition helps companies keep the brand engagement and revenue of the company increasing. Think of Facebook and Instagram, Disney and Pixar/Marvel, or Amazon and Ring. These companies are brands consumers know and trust. To rebrand is time consuming and costly to the company. It wasn't broken, why fix it?

Selling Your Company

Selling your business outright is an additional option. Some individual investors look for opportunities to buyout an owner and take on full ownership of a business. There are more non-investors looking to purchase businesses than ever before. This is great because there are more baby boomers looking to sell their businesses. Due to generational changes, business owners are less likely to pass their businesses down to their children. Generations are choosing other careers of interest over keeping up with the family legacy.

There are savvy business professionals who have experience in certain industries and buying a business makes more sense to them than starting one or buying into a franchise. Even though you can sell your company to a family member or businessperson there are other options to sell your business.

Creating an employee-owned business is an option. All employees of the company will pull together and purchase and operate the company. This is great for many companies because now the employees have additional incentives to work more efficiently to keep the business thriving. Employee-owned companies have higher moral and business brand loyalty; something which takes years to develop. Publix and Lifetouch Photography Company are two of the most popular employee-owned companies today.

Investors who buy businesses recognize immediate cash flow, a book of business, and opportunities to grow the business in other areas. The famous businessman and investor, Reginald F. Lewis, believed it made little sense to start a company when you could just buy one. More investors are feeling the same way.

Selling your business requires important legal agreements. Sometimes, the company owner stays with the company for a certain period to create a smooth transition. Other times, the expectation is an abrupt departure of the business. Owners can still possess a stake in the company for a smaller buyout. The agreement must be solid, and all parties must understand their obligations.

Not every founder has to sell the business. A co-founder could choose a buyout for their stake in the business. What will this mean for the other co-founder(s) of the business? They'll remain founders and have an equity stake in the business. Just because a buyout happens doesn't mean the purchaser owns the company. You need an iron clad legal agreement in the buyout by stating responsibilities, ownership stake, and what the equity stake means to the newcomer and other parties involved. How will everyone work together with the original founder gone and this additional person in the mix?

Recapitalization

Recapitalization is also an option but seldom mentioned with exit strategy. This is partially because it creates an exit strategy for the investor more than the founder. The purpose of recapitalization is to modify your debt-to-equity ratio. It's a strategy resulting in increased or reduced debt. When you as a founder look to provide an exit strategy for your investors, you buyout their shares and distribute it back to the business. This reduces the debt the of the business and provides the investor a nice payday. It also relieves them from all obligations they held as a board member. The founder/business doesn't have to buyout all investors, only specific shareholders. A wise founder will look to buyout shareholders who are dead weight for the company. Those are shareholders who provide no additional value or chose to ride the bandwagon with the growth of the company by injecting capital but contributed nothing else to the company.

Liquidation

Liquidation is a dire consequence of poor business decisions or a declining industry. This strategy calls for the founder selling all business assets for the purpose of exiting and recouping as much money as possible. They'll also provide themselves with large dividends or salaries as a way of bleeding the company dry before closing up shop. If you have a board of directors, they will not allow this to be your exit strategy. If the company is managed properly, you will receive greater returns and a better reputation from just selling.

Exit strategies, though complicated, must be tactical. The founder and investor must come in with an end goal in mind. Exiting is a natural part of the startup process, however it happens. Ask yourself what makes the most sense for you.

Intro to Part II

Congratulations, you've completed the first half of the book! The second half has a different format. You will use this for your reference going forward in your startup or as an investor. It's a list of questions ask by an investor after your pitch and throughout the life of the investor/founder relationship.

This half will include five main business areas and questions specific to products, services, and industries. Keep this as your lifelong reference guide and you won't go wrong.

Chapter Eight: Team/Founders

Introduction

Exploration of your founder and team is the bait on the hook of investing. Do they possess the right domain knowledge? Are they entrenched in the industry? Do they hold magnificent vision and foresight to keep the business going? Do they possess external support from family, friends, and/or their advisors? Who are the individuals who are most influential in their decisions to keep the startup going? The experience, domain knowledge, and skill set of the founder are important, along with their flexibility to do the job. What gaps in knowledge does the founder portray, and how has the founder filled the gaps? These questions are important to answer while creating your team.

Founders

It's important the investor knows who you are as a founder. Are you a risk taker? Do you influence your team? Are you a visionary? Don't worry about the hard skills you feel you're lacking in your business. Your pitch doesn't focus on a lack of skills, it focuses on the problem you're solving and the potential to grow it into a company. Hard skills such as understanding finance and marketing are solvable. You can always bring in experts and partners to support the lack of hard skills. It's your soft skills an investor is trying to gauge. It is how we determine a successful founder. How you present your pitch and how you control the room can tell a lot about a founder. Your attitude and confidence reveal your passion for what you're doing and your ability to captivate an audience with other investors, partners, and major companies. The ability to present well excites an investor. There were many brilliant orators throughout time, however, consider some current greats:

- Marc Benioff
- Steve Jobs
- Robert F. Smith
- Richard Branson
- Larry Ellison

These founders are all great visionaries who present(ed) well and charm(ed) their audiences. They leave their followers wanting to know more. Steve Jobs created a cult of followers who stand in endless lines all around the nation to buy the newest iPhone. You may not embody a Steve Jobs, but you can still acquire the same skills to deliver a great message. I suggest joining a local Toastmasters club if you fear public speaking or feel you want to improve your delivery. It's an elite organization with many chapters all over the world. It's an exceptional place to network and creates a practice stage for pitching and presentations.

Let's start with general questions to the founder.

Why did you start this business?

Alternate Question: Why did you choose this business or industry?

It's an opportune time for you as the founder(s) to tell your story and show your genuine passion behind the business. If you partner with co-founders, it also solidifies your bond. If your stories and passions align, it strengthens your business value. It says you all are in the company together through the trials. It also says you believe in what you are doing.

Example: An impressive example of a startup story is the start of Microsoft with Bill Gates and Paul Allen as founders. Bill and Paul were childhood friends who even attended the same college. While walking through the business district around the Harvard campus, Paul saw the cover of Popular Magazine which showcased the Altair 8800 microcomputer. This excited Paul and he immediately purchased the magazine and raced through campus to show Bill. After talking about the technology, they saw an opportunity to use BASIC (Beginners' All-purpose Symbolic Instruction Code) as the programming language on the Altair. They called Altair's manufacturing company and offered to provide a demo of how BASIC could help their computers. Once they agreed, they went to California, successfully demoed their idea. They received an offer to do business with the manufacturer. Soon after, they both quit Harvard University and founded Microsoft.

How did you come up with this idea?

Like asking why you entered this industry, speak specifically about why you are the right CEO. What is your experience and how did you develop a passion for this idea? Once again, this is an excellent time to tell your story. Stories draw people in and improve your credibility and level of influence. Unlike the story on why you created your business, this is likely simple and straight to the point story. Make sure it includes the problem you are trying to solve and how you solved it. It's not just about you, bring it back to the product or service you provide.

Examples: "My wife and I debate all the time about what's considered 'done' when washing clothes. I say if they're washed and dried, they're done. 'Done' for her means you fold the clothes and put them in drawers. I hate folding clothes, especially when there are a lot of them. I created [insert product idea] so I would never need to fold my clothes again!"

"Ice cream has always been my favorite food! Living in Florida, I go to my favorite ice cream shop about a mile from my house. I always buy a double scoop of chocolate ice cream with a cone. The problem is, when I'm conversing with friends, there's no place to sit my cone and if I hold it, it just melts in my hand. I knew I could solve this simple issue and created [insert product]."

"I knew so many friends who wanted to invest in [insert business], however, they did not know how to invest. I even wanted to invest in those businesses. I decided this is easier than [insert process]. From there I developed this idea and plan I knew could help my friends and me."

You develop the right product/service, and you possess the capability of finding a unique and profitable consumer need.

What keeps you up at night?

This is a question asked by a very interested investor who either doesn't know much about the business/industry you're in or is testing your understanding of the industry. This is one of my favorite questions to ask a founder. The unique answers provided by savvy founders amaze me. Very few times am I underwhelmed, however there are some underwhelming responses. These are not the answers you want to provide:

- Continuous unknown failures
- Not receiving traction
- Lack of sales
- No marketing
- So many copycats
- Hard time acquiring funding

Avoid using these generic answers. Dive deeper into the above list. Dive as deep as you can to find the one major threat to your business. It must make you uncomfortable. If you're having an issue with diving deeper, use the Five Why's technique.

Example: Let's look at two examples of using the Five Whys.

Lack of Sales

- Why #1: I need to increase sales.
- Why #2: I need to increase cash flow.
- Why #3: My margins are low.
- Why #4: The market is competitive for new startups.
- Why #5: We must gain more reach and show clients how our services provide a better ROI for their business.

Translating this into a response: What keeps me up at night is how our potential customers will view our alternative method. Though it increases their company's ROI better than our competitors, the market is still competitive. To combat this, our margins are low so we can grab a foothold into our target market. I believe once we achieve some traction, we can increase our margin, cash flow, and sales.

Hard time acquiring funding

- Why #1: I need funding and cannot obtain it.
- Why #2: I know little about acquiring funding.
- Why #3: I haven't been able to put the footwork into learning about how to acquire funding properly.
- Why #4: I'm a one-man band and I'm focusing on the product and business operations. My capacity is full.
- Why #5: I'm new to entrepreneurship and I do not know how to bring on employees without losing money.

Translating this into a response: What keeps me up at night is not being able to scale my business without going broke. I'm working to acquire funding, but this is an area foreign to me. Because I'm focusing so much on my product, I do not feel I have the time and expertise to bring on additional employees.

If you look at this example, the actual problem keeping this founder up at night is the fear of being able to scale properly. Do not feel you cannot say, "I don't know" how to do something. It's expected that a founder won't know everything. Someone else can fill those gaps as you grow. Investors already understand your background, and it's not your job as a founder to know how to do everything. It also takes time and support to obtain knowledge in many areas of business.

What are your aspirations as a founder?

This sounds like a corny interview question, but it could shed more light on who you are as a person and founder. It doesn't have to include an individual in your industry. It doesn't have to consist of a famous person. It doesn't even have to include a specific person at all. I often view founders as visionaries and risk-takers. By knowing your aspirations, I can draw similarities throughout the rest of my relationship with you.

Example: I interviewed a founder her answer included the entrepreneurs she aspired to emulate.

"I aspire to live by my set of core values. There are many entrepreneurs I've met on my journey who began like me. They constantly worked hard and took any job available to bring in revenue. Once they gained the right traction, they narrowed their business capabilities allowing them to focus solely on their passions, spirituality, and health. Their time is THEIR TIME, and they don't change or skew their core values to meet the demands of their business. They still touch thousands of lives. Those individuals are who I aspire to be."

Who do you least want to be like?

This question from my experience always throws a founder off their game. It's not often I hear this question but there's usually a pause before an awkward answer. If the pitch and follow-up questions did not go well, an investor may ask this question. This question, followed-up by unwelcoming body language could mean you're not obtaining investment from this pitch. Sound the alarm if asked this during a pitch unless the investor has already invested capital. It's likely you've lost the chance for investment. If they've already invested money into your business, they're asking this for another reason.

When developing a relationship with an active investor, they become like family or a trusted advisor. If they ask, "Who you least want to be like?" it's their way of finding pain points and using them for motivation. If a founder tells an investor, they least want to be like someone who constantly disappointed them throughout life, a motivator for the founder may be to not disappoint family, friends, or customers. It will drive them to work harder and remember why they need to keep going. An investor can always pull on this string if they feel the founder is losing motivation.

What's been the most motivating moment in your business?

It doesn't matter if its big moments or brief moments. It's important to think of unique, empowering, and motivating times in your entrepreneurial journey. As founders, sometimes you quit or experience difficult roadblocks you must overcome.

Example: I remember a time right before beta testing an online service when someone hacked my servers. I spent the whole weekend rebuilding, and I quickly decided to not just have a backup site but use a different hosting company as my backup. I replicated my design and built an operation manual around switching to the backup server if we ever experienced server issues with my primary hosting business again. The beta testing went off with only one minor hitch, and the users loved the platform. The failure motivated me because for the first time I felt like a true founder. I solved the problem but also created a business continuity plan around my IT infrastructure.

Where is your headquarters located?

During a due diligence event, an eCommerce business with an American founder seemed promising. The startup obtained quick traction, and its products were selling at an exponential rate. We later found out the "American company's" headquarters was in China. There's not necessarily anything wrong with this, however laws, rules, and regulations are different for startups in other countries. Investors have to be cognizant of those rules or contract experienced people who work with out-of-country investments.

I now ask this question when founders don't state it in their pitch. I need to know where they are from and where their business is located. If you're doing business globally, it requires additional due diligence. As mentioned earlier, your due diligence process can change depending on the company. A review of legal documents will require thoroughness if the company is not in your home country. It could change the deal structure or ruin the deal. As a founder, upfront disclosure about this is beneficial before starting the due diligence process.

Why are you the right person to bet on to achieve this vision?

As a founder, figure this out because investors will pose this question to you and themselves. A lot of founders struggle with this answer. You've already provided the investor with your story. This may mean your story is not enough or they foresee someone else as a better founder. Obviously you are building this business and working hard to grow it, but it's important for an investor that you are in this for the right reasons, you have the right skills to grow the company, and you want to see this company to IPO or sell. What value do you bring to your business others cannot? Your history in a specific industry is very important. If another person developed your business, who and would they show more successful than you? Why? This is what you must ask yourself. Sometimes it's not just about having passion but doing the work to place your imprint as a founder and/or CEO into the industry. Also, the right leader possesses the mental fortitude to work hard and build the right network around them.

A company I invested in possessed the kind of founders most investors only dream of. The founders not only thought of a superb idea and developed a roadmap to implement the idea, but they also possessed a foothold in the industry in several states. They created an organization around the industry and were on several boards in their industry. Being this active wasn't enough for them. They lobbied for revised laws in their industry, and they partnered with state agencies to change how the industry works.

Just because you may not the right person for the job today doesn't mean you cannot make yourself the right person for the job.

What does your close network look like?

Alternate Question: Who is part of your tribe?
Founders need to keep mentors and advisors, but it's those who support you from the background that mean the most on your startup journey. Your tribe/crew/entrepreneurial circles must consist of powerful individuals. Not powerful as in millionaire and billionaire but powerful as in they can provide you with the support to help you grow your company. As an investor, the founder's tribe is who they talk to about their business and receives advice from. This is very important. You'll read a different variation of this question later in the book, but just remember the individuals who the founder associates with directly affect them and their decision making.

What motivates you?

This is a positive question. Investors want to know what motivates a founder because everyone has a different motivation. Many entrepreneurs have multiple motivations whether it be their kids, helping people, or their personal story. The most powerful motivation means the investor can use it to push you, the founder, to keep going when startup life gets rough. This is an opportunity for the founder to solidify who they are and how you and your business are a perfect match.

Example: I asked a member of my entrepreneurial circle this question in an interview. His answer was powerful.

"I'm motivated by the opportunity of life. Surviving cancer at a young age placed my passions in perspective. It took me on a spiritual journey, helping me realize my love for helping people build wealth meant more than working for a company. It created an awakening in me like a ball of fire in a closed pot. I live my life with this spirit, and I want to share it with everyone I encounter."

Now, your motivation doesn't have to be this deep. I must say, if I just met him, I would have become a customer or investor immediately.

Are you working on your business idea full-time?

Based on the stage you are in with your business; this question could lead an investor and founder in different directions. Some investors may think it's smart you have a job and you're also working on your business. Others may think you're not fully invested and need to quit your job to focus on your business. Understand the stance of the investor before pitching them. Have a reason you believe in your stance if you two are on opposite sides of the fence.

Example: Wayne Lynwood received the same question when pitching his fintech business. His business generated revenue however, he still maintained his current job. The investor he pitched felt his job prevented him from scaling his business. Here is Wayne's response:

"I struggle with this decision every day. After doing some evaluation, it is more about the profit than the revenue. Today, I am pouring my money and the business's profits back into the business. With your funding, I can gain more traction and hit my goal numbers to quit my job and possess enough runway to increase my sales by 35% over the next 4 months. This would allow me to pay myself a salary, profit, and continue to grow the business."

How do you make your living now?

Sometimes your employment status is not clear. As entrepreneurs, we like to act as if we do not have any other job. If you are working on your business full time, this is a common question. I would answer this question and the previous question together if asked. This will close unnecessary doors leading to more follow-up questions.

The response from your investor will present you with a better idea of the mindset your investor possesses. Some investors would want a full-time entrepreneur. This is seldom negotiable at first. If you're working another job, an investor may think you're not fully invested in your startup. Do not let this sway you to quit your job. How you make a living for you and your family is important and maybe this investor is not the right one for you.

Other investors like to know you're hustling to fund your business or you're working eight hours at work and another eight or more hours on your business everyday. Speak openly to your investors about this. Every situation is unique, and the investor needs to understand your situation.

Have you founded or owned any other businesses?

Investors want to gauge your level of entrepreneurial maturity, and your age does not matter. It's all about business polish. What do you know and what have you done? If this is your first business, fine. By asking you about your track record, the investors make assumptions, ultimately helping you through the rest of your due diligence period.

Follow-up Questions:

- If so, does the business still exist?
- If so, how well is the business doing?
- If so, will running this business take away from working on the business I'm investing in?

Do you have any other ideas?

This is a positive sign. If you have not already expressed you have other products or services coming down the pipeline correlating with your business, an investor asking if you possess other ideas is typically a sign they envision a long-term partnership with you. At the least, they want to. Sometimes, an investor can recognize a visionary and innovator. As opportunists, they will invest in you as a founder of your current company with the firm belief you'll develop other dynamic and investable products. I know some investors who have put in insignificant amounts of money for a startup just to obtain first dibs on what the founder creates next.

How many hours a week do you work on your business?

Even though some successful entrepreneurs take a note from Tim Ferriss's book *The 4-Hour Workweek*, most investors like to know you're spending a lot of time on your business. This is especially the case for a startup. Many entrepreneurs work sixty or more hours and if you're an entrepreneurial maniac like Grant Cardone, you're working at least ninety-five hours a week. There's no correct amount of time you must work. It's about how productive you are.

What does a typical day look like with you?

This is a common question for an investor to understand how you work. If you're working four hours or ninety-five hours, investors are interested to know you're using your time wisely and being productive. If you work at either of these extremes, telling an investor you "do a lot" or you "do everything" in a typical day, will make them lose trust in you as a founder. This is not the time to waffle. Layout a typical timeline because you know what you do daily.

Example: Every weekday I wake up at 5:15 a.m. and start my day with breakfast and reading. By 6:30 I'm at the gym and then back home to work from about 8:45 to 5 in the evening. Once my children go to sleep at 8:30 p.m., my wife and I have an hour and a half together then I go back to work until 11:00 p.m. before going to sleep and starting over again.

Are you paying yourself?

There's no right or wrong answer to this unless you're paying yourself a ridiculous amount of money and your business is suffering. This is a moment where you say "yes" or "no," and if you are, let the investor know how much you pay yourself. Sometimes founders who are not paying themselves and have no other source of income are unhappy, worn out, and desperate. Investors will sense it and will either capitalize on it from a valuation perspective or do what I consider "the right thing" and force the founder to pay themselves as an agreement in closing the investment deal.

If your business failed, what would you do?

This is a question I've watched founders struggle with. I've heard founders say they will not fail, and failure is not an option. I've experienced others provide no answer at all unless you consider "I don't know" a proper answer. This is one of the few times an investor does not! As you read this, I challenge you to come up with an answer other than, "This business won't fail," and "I don't know."

Example: "I've been an entrepreneur for most of my life. I have several other ideas, but I'm most passionate about this one. When I first started this, I thought about how my product could keep me from becoming homeless in my younger years. It helps families in under-served areas increase their economic mobility. Now if this failed, I have other ideas to help the same families and create similar opportunities. My passion for what I'm doing is beyond this product. I don't expect it will cause my business to fail. If it does, I'll keep fighting the good fight in what I believe to help those who need it the most."

How do you define success for the business?

The answer to this question is up to you. Investors appreciate a quantitative response. How is your business success defined in the form of quality, growth, time, or money? Based on your preferences and vision, your definition of success looks similar to one or more of these examples:

- Helping [insert metric] families in under-served communities change their lives.
- Serving [insert metric] homeless veterans monthly/quarterly/yearly.
- Steadily earning [insert metric] in profit every quarter.
- Making [insert metric] in revenue.
- Being a globally recognized business in [insert industry].
- Making [insert metric] in revenue.
- Providing for my family without worries of paying for essentials.
- Being able to have at least [insert amount] dollars in the bank.
- In [insert years] years I want to make a million dollars.
- In [insert years] years I want to sell the business for [insert amount] dollars.

No matter what the answer, use your real answer, not just what you think you want the investors to hear. Some investors can sense when you're being untruthful by providing a canned answer. Find your definition, make it into a business goal, and work towards it every day.

What is your favorite part of being an entrepreneur?

Once again, there's no wrong answer. It is a common question for investors who have already determined they will invest in your business. I often hear something like flexibility or freedom. They do not make entrepreneurs who want to work for "the man."

Example: Kyle Earling gave us a great and concise response. It is a variation of what I've heard many entrepreneurs say.

Kyle worded it like this, "Entrepreneurship is challenging and never the same. Not only do you meet prominent businessmen and women, but you finally meet you and what you can truly accomplish. I've pushed myself and learned skills I never thought I would need or possess. That's my favorite part of being an entrepreneur."

In this message, Kyle let the investors know he enjoys challenging work, and he's adaptable to change. It also shows he's not afraid to "roll up his sleeves and get dirty" with the rest of the employees in his business. He also mentioned he loved leading employees in his business.

Team & Management Structure

Who are the key employees?

Key employees are very important in a startup. Many times, they are individuals who provide a major contribution to your company. Those folks are often your first employees and/or co-founders. They believe in your product or service and will work for free because they understand the potential. If you are not paying your key employee(s), are you at least providing them equity? Some angels or VC will require you to offer your key employees equity as part of funding your round. Work hard to keep your key employees. They are the ones who are growing your business.

Any existing board members?

Board members make a difference when investing. Every single time I have invested in a startup with a set of board members, it has been important to meet them face-to-face and understand how they feel about the business. Board of directors invest time into pointing startups in the right direction. This is a significant investment in time. It's even stronger when the board members have invested their own money into the startup. Board members also have distinct key qualities and a solid vision to help drive the business. I was given advice on what type of people I should structure my board with many years ago and I still use this same structure today. A board should resemble the abilities (not necessarily the titles) as follows:

- Lawyer or Doctor - Someone able to consume and analyze sizable sums of information in a brief period.
- Business Consultant or Former Entrepreneur - Someone who knows holistically about business and can provide the right guidance to keep your company moving. They are also someone who has been where you are and understand your struggles.
- Public Relations or Marketing Specialist - Someone who can provide direction to make your brand memorable.
- Industry Specialist - Someone who can help you define your strategy as it relates to mapping out the future of the industry you're in and open doors and builds bridges to the communities you serve who can help your business grow.
- IT or Process Guru - Someone who can make sure you're streamlining your operations or keeping in mind how automation will make your business more efficient. These experts are more forward-thinking than others on your board.

What is your hiring plan?

An investor wants to know if you think about future growth. If your business is already running or about to launch, have you forecasted the sales, revenue, and profit? The only way to forecast profit is to take into account the employees you need to hire for your company. If you're still in the concept stage, it's common to not know the answer just yet. If you've built your business plan, have this information and a roadmap to hiring based on your financial forecast.

Example: "As a three-founder team, we've developed specific roles and responsibilities for ourselves. We've realized we can produce 325 products per month and handle all administrative and logistics tasks. Once we supersede that amount, we'll need to bring on a part-time assistant and one full-time person to fulfill orders. This will keep us lean and optimize our production."

Who in this organization is most replaceable?

The translation to this question is "how lean is your business from the viewpoint of talent?" Do you have the right number of employees? Can you downsize? Do you have dead weight in your business? Did you just hire your buddy because you they volunteered to work for free? Are you making the right hiring decisions?

Working lean is always important. As a startup founder, you want to exhaust ways of reducing cost but still deliver a quality product or service. Having employees on the payroll is one of your priciest expenses. Investors want to know how you manage money (especially how you will manage their money) and if you look for ways to make your business lean and efficient.

What experience do you have in this industry?

As a Founder, it's helpful to possess some experience or knowledge into the business you're working. Founders build many startups through a problem they experienced themselves. As stated in the previous section, having a strategic foothold in your industry can open doors and present your company insight on how to grow and plan for future growth. The founder must involve themselves in industry work outside of the startup, and they must influence their team to be active in the industry too. They should take part in associations, take time to gain industry knowledge, and collaborate on ways to make the company better. It also helps to join groups in which their customers are members. When hiring, searching for someone in your industry may remove some of these roadblocks other new businesses may have trouble overcoming. It's never too late to gain this industry experience so start now.

Example: I met a founder in the real estate industry who ran a rapidly growing residential real estate business. Her team comprised eight employees who performed various duties from administrative assistant, analyst, property manager, and builder. She required each team member to become members of a related organization. The company also paid their memberships. The only stipulation is they were to remain active members and any recent information learned they would present during their monthly team meeting.

By doing this, she could spend her time learning about the industry and also focus more on sales and new development. On the other side, the team felt invested in the business. They contributed and witnessed how the information progressed the company. They felt like they played an extensive role in the company. Their bonuses also showed this.

Do you have a co-founder?

Having a co-founder is sometimes a strong preference for an investor. It is perceived having a co-founder makes for a stronger business. There's no "one-man (woman) show," but there's undeniable support leading your company. If you do not have one, an investor may want to know why not.

Who are the founders?

If you have founders and they have not met your investor, a formal introduction must happen. Just like the investor meeting your board members, they must obtain face time with the co-founder(s) to make this deal successful.

Who did you choose not to include as a co-founder and why?

Alternate Question: How did you choose the founders of your company?
Example: This is a unique question one of my colleagues asked during a due diligence session. The founders of this startup created their business with ten individuals, they considered however only three of them founders. There were several reasons there were only three founders, and it based all of them on the individual preferences of the team members.

1. The title of the founder or leader in the company is not desired.
2. Some preferred to work as a 9-5 employee and not manage the day-to-day operations and strategy.

3. Others felt they did not have the business mindset or created value as a founder.

The consensus from all ten team members revealed the three founders designated, deserved to be the founders for the job. The other seven members receive equity in the startup because of their dedication to the team and as compensation since they were not receiving pay.

Can we buy out any of the co-founders?

For a founder, this is likely a positive sign. It means your investor wants more equity or wants to free up more equity in your company. Sometimes a co-founder may not bring value to the business itself and the investor may view it more beneficial to the company to buy the founder out, leaving them no control in the business and possibly no position in the business. This may sound harsh, but the investor is not doing this selfishly but in the best interest of the company.

What if they want to buy you out? This is your baby, and you may not desire to give up all your equity now or at all. Your goal could be to keep the business and your vision clear for the future of the company. An investor offering to buy you out may be a sign you need to increase your valuation and at least hold on a little longer to your business. Know the value of your business and make a sound decision whether it's better to sell now, later, or at all.

Are you paying your team?

If you're not paying your team, I commend you as a founder who can build a tribe. It says a lot about a founder who can create a team and not pay them. This is where the power of influence is strong, and it shows people like the founder enough to work for free even if only part-time. It also shows other believe in the vision of your startup. If you're not paying your team, an investor will want to know when will they receive payment and how much of the investment will go to them?

What gaps do you have in your team dynamics right now?

Some investors take on the job of helping the founder staff their team. Even better, they help find experienced partners to fill gaps. Gaps in team dynamics or capabilities can lead to greater inefficiencies as the team scales.

Are there any other people who may claim ownership or responsibility for your idea(s)?

The startup world is not always smooth and happy. When coming up with your idea, you may run it by friends and family. They'll provide their suggestions and opinions. If you use any suggestions, you can risk a person feeling you owe them something as your company becomes successful. Another scenario would include a company starting with co-founders, then the co-founders split to start their own companies for whatever reason. One co-founder may keep moving forward with the idea and then when growth comes, the past co-founders claim they deserve some kind of compensation for helping the business grow.

Example: The most popular example happened with Facebook. The Winklevoss Brothers claim Mark Zuckerberg stole their idea and sued him for $140 million for the idea of the infamous Facebook.

Now, the three of them were not co-founders but the claims were valid no matter if the idea was stolen or not.

Chapter Nine: Commercial

The Business

What does the name of your business mean?

Names with unique stories behind them, helps create brand recognition. This engages the investor and draws them into you and your thoughtfulness as a founder. If you think of companies like Google, Samsung, or Starbucks, they seem like strange names for internet, cellphone, and coffee companies however they all have their own story and message.

Examples: Co-founder Larry Page of Google misspelled what he meant to write as "Googol" and the name stuck. Samsung means "Three Stars" in Korean and the founder, Lee Byung-chul, wanted the company to last forever like stars in the sky. The three stars stood for something powerful, big, and bright in Korean culture. Starbucks experimented with several names. Through a series of word association, they went from "ST" to "Starbo" to "Starbuck" and then Starbucks. Starbuck was also the name of the first mate on the whaling ship in the novel Moby-Dick.

Names like John's Consulting are obvious. When considering you're building a brand, creativity is important. One of my companies, Groopwork, seems like a misspelling, however it has a unique meaning. The story intrigues people. Some investors may not care about your name, but others strategically ask to learn more about the story of the business, and the way you think.

How long have you been in business?

Investors correlate the time you've been in business with the traction you've made. If you've been in business for five years and have only made $5,000, this is a red flag for investing. This creates more questions why you only generated such an insignificant amount of revenue. There's no perfect number to gauge where a company should be each year, but revenue is an important factor in companies who have already launched their product or service. If you're concerned about this as a founder, be proactive by providing an answer to your potential investor with the assumption they will ask.

What is your business's unique advantage?

Alternate Question: Have you invented something not easily replicated?

What is proprietary about your product or service and what is your unique value proposition? Go back to your business model canvas or business plan to review this information.

Example: Lee Davidson created her boutique consulting firm. She became known as the best in her local market and her name grew quickly as the person who could solve culture change in small businesses. She designed a proprietary assessment to gauge the culture of these businesses, but she also created a proven and proprietary process framework to mitigate ninety percent of identified risks for these companies within eight months, once implementation began.

How are you going to turn this business into a brand?

Before answering this question, you must understand brand and brand engagement. Brand is not just a logo, it's what current and future customers think about when they view your logo or hear your company's name. A brand portrays what a customer expects from your business. A prominent example is the company Apple. While the company name and logo would mean nothing in a "Pre-Apple" world, the company still has a brand today. When you see Apple, you think of experience and innovation. A brand is what you want clients to think and see.

Brand engagement goes deeper. It's how a client emotionally connects to your brand. There should be a commitment to the point they would not buy from anyone else under any circumstance.

Examples: Using the example of Apple again, customers become emotionally attached to the brand, and so passionate about their dedication to the brand they're called "The Cult of Apple." They've created evangelist out of their customers. Those customers then convince others to buy and they become an evangelist. I cannot tell you how many times in a month someone recommends I switch to an Apple product.

We met a potential founder we wanted to invest in. When asked, "What would you do with the money?" he quickly said, rebrand my company. Since "brand" means so many things, we dug deeper to find he didn't know what "brand" really meant. His lack of understanding could have been costly to him, but I ended up helping him find the right brand engagement firm. He now knows what full service branding and brand engagement means.

Is this the original business idea you thought of when you founded your business?

I love this question because I receive all kinds of answers. It takes the investor on a journey of how the company evolved and the business decisions the founder made to get there. Investors want to know you're focused, opportunistic, and flexible. It's okay if you have pivoted, rebranded, or even created a business based on your original findings. Some of the greatest companies have done the same thing.

Examples:

- Twitter (formerly Odeo) began as a network to help individuals find podcasts.
- Starbucks first sold espresso makers and coffee beans to its customers.
- Instagram (formerly Burbn) became developed as a check-in app having photos and games.
- Pinterest (formerly Tote) erected as an ecommerce company to search, track, and save fashion collections.
- Suzuki auto and motorcycle maker first manufactured looms for the silk industry in Japan.

If these examples are not to your satisfaction, you can find many more famous companies out there who have done the same. They did it to stay relevant and build their companies. Pivoting can be a sign to the investor a founder is not only a visionary but can foresee changes in an industry and knows when, where, and how to pivot the company. This is only if the pivot was a smart decision.

Example: I attended a pitch contest two years ago and one judge followed the history of one founder competing (obviously an unfair advantage to the other founders pitching). The judge knew the founder pivoted his business based on creating an MVP and realizing his customers wanted something different and ended up way more lucrative for his company. The founder explained how he pivoted to a model using the same customer base but for a greater customer need. This one question became the prime reason he won the contest. Later he pivoted again to a completely different business.

Pivots can typically show how a founder's business has revealed a new customer segment or synergy of capabilities across multiple businesses. It could also mean you're an indecisive founder and you pivot when things get tough in your business. It shows intelligence to present and justify why you pivoted to eliminate investors having a negative perception of you.

What are some standard business roadblocks in your industry?

Investors know every industry has its roadblocks. If you tell an investor, there are no industry roadblocks, they know you have not done enough research on your industry. They may feel you're not invested in the company and you're not becoming a thought leader in your industry.

How do you keep up with trends in your industry?

Founders must keep up with trends in their industry. Trends can ultimately alter the way a business works with its customer. The expansion of Amazon caused grocery stores to offer delivery and parking lot pickup for customers. The uprising in blogs and podcasts changed how media outlets report the news.

There are several effortless ways to track trends in your industry:

1. Follow a daily cadence of researching in media.
2. Set Google Alerts or Google Trends to discover industry news related to you.
3. Create custom news boards on your mobile device.
4. Use a feed aggregator or reader to follow your favorite industry sites.
5. Follow social media mentions and/or hashtags.

What other company do you aspire your business to model?

We answered a similar question in a previous section. However, this is not founder related, it's related to the business. Have you looked at how other business are operating? If you have, what company would you want to emulate? Comparing yourself operationally, technologically, and culturally is not a poor strategy. One mistake we make as entrepreneurs is we always feel the need to recreate a perfectly functioning wheel. It shouldn't take away from your value, and it allows you to model certain parts of your business after companies who do it well. Companies do this all the time; it's called benchmarking.

What companies wouldn't you model?

If you're already thinking of how other companies operate, you're likely thinking of what they do poorly. As an entrepreneur, I am constantly evaluating companies in which I'm a customer of. What are they doing well? Is there customer service consistent? Are their operations flawless? Do I always receive the same quality product or service? What companies do you feel are not doing well in the industry and outside of the industry? Are they performing antiquated processes? Investors want to know you pay attention to other businesses.

How does your company's strategy help you achieve your ultimate vision?

Vision differs from strategy. Strategy is the roadmap to get to your vision. There is no single answer to this. There are strategies in all areas of your business such as marketing, launching, scaling, logistics, and product development.

Example: Tesla's goal is "to create the most compelling car company of the 21st century by driving the world's transition to electric vehicles." Merge this with its founder's, Elon Musk's vision to become the biggest car manufacturer, they designed a unique strategy to get there and look to be succeeding.

In 2003, when Tesla started, they took a different strategy than most technology and automobile manufacturers would take. Instead of building a free or low-priced MVP, they flipped the scale to launch a high-end, luxury, electric sports car, the Roadster. It doesn't seem like a $200,000 car would lead to Musk's vision, however it sparked a lot of attention and led to more affordable models being created. Today, Tesla outpaces all other electric car models in sales and provides models well under the $200,000 price tag.

What does it take to build and scale a company in this category from scratch?

Companies in a saturated market need to know this answer. Investors will quickly sniff out a startup who is entering a saturated market. A startup developing a new social networking service or one that is in the food industry must create a strategy to stand out and be successful.

Example: McDonald's brand redefined the meaning of fast food. By putting systems in place to produce quality food products while the customer stood at the window paying for their food was unheard of at the time. Though it seems archaic now, there were no drive through windows. You still had to park, get out of your car, and walk up to a window and make an order. McDonald's unique processes not only created a unique value proposition, but it created a brand other chain modeled themselves from.

What is your exit strategy?

This is an important question for an investor looking for a big payday at the end of the investment engagement. Investors make the most money during the buy/sell of the startup. Investors also want to know what type of investor you are. Are you a "starting pitcher" who will setup the startup, grow it, then move on? Those are serial entrepreneurs. They like to hop from one company to another. Are you a small business owner? Someone who will stick with the company forever and remain CEO?

At the seed stage of a company, most founders have not considered their exit strategy. New founders have not even figure out what kind of founder they want to be. They're not even looking to exit at all. Exiting a company you've built is almost like sending your child off to college. You leave your wins, losses, and all the related emotions with the company. It's difficult to let go. If you're extremely early in the startup stage, investors may not want to hear you having thoughts of selling your business. This may provide thoughts the founder is not fully committed and the business is likely to fail. If you have aspirations of selling, focus on growth and don't worry about exiting your business.

Business Model

I use the words "business" and "company" interchangeably throughout this book. In the remaining questions within this chapter, I will distinguish the unique meanings of both. This will change how you answer the questions.

A ***Business*** builds a product and puts it on the market for sale. On top of a product, a business comprises people, processes, and resources allowing you to sell the product. Even with a key person gone, a business must still operate effectively. Otherwise, it's just a product.

A ***Company*** is an organization running one or more businesses. For a startup, it's likely you haven't reached the level to become a "real" company. If you have, you are not looking for funding and would not need to acquire capital unless you need to acquire funding for an extensive capital project to expand (which doesn't normally happen in the angel investment world). Consider a company to be more like a billion dollar corporation.

Nice product/service. Tell me how this is a business?

Now you understand the definition of a business, this is the time where you talk about the people, processes, and tools you are using to sell your product. How do you plan to sustain operations and if you aren't sustaining, what are your plans for improvement? Selling a few products doesn't necessarily mean you're an investable business. It could be a side hustle only.

Which specific marketing channels are you using?

Going back to the business model canvas, it's important to understand the most optimal way to reach your customers. In today's market, most companies use social media avenues. No matter what avenue you chose, let the investor know how big the customer segment is in each channel. Why are you using these marketing channels?

Through market research, you can justify why you are using the channels. This is how you will let the investor know how big the segment is in each channel. The answer tells how much you know your customer.

Example: I met a marketing guru several years ago who started a business for lawyers. To market, the likely marketing channel would be LinkedIn or some kind of law journal. It was not the case at all. Through customer discovery, they realized after a long day's work, lawyers tended to go home, have dinner with their family, then scroll through Facebook for hours in bed before going to sleep. That was their way of winding down. The business saw an opportunity and through Facebook Ad campaigns, they managed to accelerate the growth of their business.

What is your Plan B if these sales channels are interrupted?

Many entrepreneurs use social media as a sales and marketing channel. What happens if your primary social media companies go out of business, deletes your user groups, or decides they do not want your type of business to market to their users? You need a backup plan. Leaving your business sales and marketing to companies who maintain all of the control is dangerous to any business.

Starting off in multiple areas and through trial and error, finding multiple sales channels can save your business.

What are your operating profit margins?

Know this simple equation and your answer is short and sweet. Profit Margin = (Net Profit / Revenue) * 100

How will scaling affect profit margins?

Sometimes scaling your business can reduce your net profit by reducing your profit margins. Founders who plan for scale tend to increase their profit margins by choosing people, processes and technology that will scale with them. These are some items reducing or increasing your profits:

- Cost of Goods
- Hiring employees
- Switching vendors
- Adding operational software
- Purchasing/leasing office space or equipment
- Increasing cost of acquiring a customer
- Research and Development

Can you tell me a story about how a customer has chosen you because of their experience with your product?

Personal stories are always better. This question lets the investor know how in-tune you are with your customer. How have you worked with the customer and have you cared to learn about their customer journey and levels of satisfaction with your product? Do you know why they will buy from you again and tell others about your business?

Example: Yolanda Flournah-Perkins, a swim teacher, tells an impressive story about a customer's daughter who grew up afraid to swim. The child's parent did everything she could to persuade her daughter to finish her swimming class. She ended up ordering Yolanda's product, Swimmie Caps®, and when the parent put it on her daughter, she seemed invincible and so happy to swim. It not only excited the parent but the child who wore the product. There are many other parents and daughters who have felt the same way when putting their children in swim lessons.

This story sparks emotion for her target market. Parents with young children afraid to swim. It also provides an understanding of what her average customer is like, what they experience, and why they buy from her.

What unique features are you working on?

Not all features will exist in your product/service today or at the launch of your business. Hopefully, you have explained to the investor the current features of your product/service. Founders have presented feature roadmaps including a list of enhancements they will make to their product over a specific timeframe. It's key to possess a thoughtfully created plan to not only enhance the product but keep the customer engagement like what Amazon does in eCommerce and Apple with the iPhone.

What other streams of revenue could you add to this?

Unlike having a growth plan, what can you do now to add a stream of income to your business? There's always a possibility of additional revenue streams in a startup business. Those could be potentially added to your growth plan as you continue to scale. FYI: Investors love subscription models, even if it isn't the primary revenue stream. It proves the business can acquire continuous cash flow.

What parts of the business are theory versus practice?

As founders, you may like to speak theoretically about what should happen in your business versus what is happening. This is a wonderful thing, but if an investor senses you are always in Dreamland, they will call you out.

Example: I met with a founder two years ago and during his pitch, he kept switching between the words "we are" and "we will." To a person who isn't analytical, it would seem his company did everything he said. I had to ask this question, "What parts of this business are you doing versus what parts does your business plan to do?" The question took him aback. He knew I caught him in what was a perceived state of efficiency. His company wasn't efficient at all. He knew what his business should do but didn't have the know how to put the processes in place. Other important traits of a founder is the ability to perform and execute.

Product and Sales

What is your minimum viable product (MVP)?

The minimum viable product is the minimum amount of value your customer will pay for. This is what you use during customer discovery to validate your idea and receive user feedback. There are a lot of big name companies who are still selling their MVPs or "betas."

Examples: Think of the Pandora streaming app. As part of their MVP, a rewind button never existed. Until this day, there's still no rewind button on the app. They realized this is not a necessity when listening to music and they were right.

Tesla's self-driving cars are being purchased by thousands of people, yet the self-driving feature is nothing but a beta test for the company to improve this feature. Though it's a cool feature for some, others are not excited about being part of an eight to ten thousand dollar autopilot test on their vehicle.

How much feedback have you received so far on your MVP?

I have seen many founders create products based on their own thoughts and experiences to find out they've missed the mark on how they designed the product or service. The investor wants to know if you have been thoughtful in creating your MVP. How did you use your customer in the process of design and after you create the MVP? Have you done focus groups, pilots, customer discovery, etc. to understand if this is what your customer wants? It shows you care about what the customer wants.

What changes have you made to your MVP based on the feedback?

This is a generic question and may mean nothing. The basic reason you receive this question is if the investor thinks you're not listening to the customer or didn't listen to the customer while building your product or service. The investor may also be a potential customer who thinks you missed the mark on developing your MVP.

How many active users/customers do you have?

This shows traction. A follow-up question, "over what period did you acquire the users/customers?" If you've obtained five users over six months, your company's traction is not sustainable unless your product is a high dollar luxury item. If you just launched, early traction sparks interest.

What is the life cycle of your users/customers?

The investor really wants to know, "How long do users stay your customer on average?" As a founder, know these numbers and ways you can improve these numbers. A founder once presented a life cycle of one day to our investment panel. The customer bought one time and never returned. As an investor, we constantly think about cash flow and how to acquire a continuous stream of income. One of my most memorable lessons when I was in sales was, "It's easier to influence existing customers to buy again". Establish a way to create loyal customers who will return to you for more products and services.

Example: As a startup founder myself, one of my companies sold training courses. Our first course lasted eight weeks and consisted of the only product in our arsenal. We knew we needed more products to keep customers coming back. Nine weeks before the launch, we developed and launched a course we could upsell to our clients to stay relevant to them.

What's the lifetime value (LTV) of a customer?

To follow up on the life cycle of your users/customer, over the life cycle, how much money do you make on average from each customer? If you only sell one product one time in the customer's life cycle, the question is easy. If you have customers on a subscription model or who purchase multiple products/services, you can find the answer through your historical sales data.

What is your churn rate?

Do you have a lot of customers who buy once and never come back? If so, what causes this? It could be because you sell a one-time buy item, your customer found a better product, you have an inferior product or service, or pushing your product is too cumbersome for the buyer. There could be plenty of other reasons, however it's your job to understand why you have a low or high churn rate.

What is your attrition rate?

Sometimes churn rate and attrition rate refers to employees or customers interchangeably. Most times, we use attrition for employees while they use churn for customers. Traction in personnel growth is also very important. Asking about attrition shows an investor how amazing or horrible the culture of the company is. If you have employees who leave, there may be a management or culture issue. If you are growing and keeping employees, it's likely individuals believe in your company and enjoy working there.

What are your current sales to-date?

Tracking sales are important, and you will probably answer this during your pitch if not directly after. This is one of the most common questions asked by an investor to a startup business. If you are not pre-revenue, sales-to-date numbers are very important.

What is your annual growth rate?

Alternate Question: What is your total growth rate?
Investors ask this to more seasoned founders. Businesses or companies who have been generating revenue for at least three years. Can you show you've been growing year over year and if you haven't, can you explain why?

Has the business's growth been linear, exponential, or steady?

This is a follow up question to your annual growth rate. You can measure this however by month, quarter, or year. Linear growth means your growth rate remained the same every year for the last three to seven years. If you grow by ten percent yearly, your growth is linear. Growing exponentially is different because there's an increase in growth every year. An excellent example is companies who double their revenue year after year. If you've gained highly exponential growth in a shorter time, it's a significant sign for an investor. Steady growth isn't really growth at all. If your business made $100,000 each year, then your revenue is steady. It doesn't (or barely) go up and down, just remains constant over time.

What has held back your growth?

I love this question as an investor. This helps understand the self-awareness of the founder of not only their business but themselves. I never receive the same answer to this question after talking to hundreds of entrepreneurs.

Can you demo (demonstrate) the product or service?

It's always smart to have something an investor can taste, touch, and/or view when explaining your company and how it works. Even with services, you can show how the service works or even allow the investor to experience the service just as a customer would.

What is the lead time to sale?

I've met founders whose companies have a business model involving what seems like endless sales lead times. It's important the company can have and maintain a good cash flow, especially if there's a long lead time to sale. This also means they must have a robust sales pipeline.

Investors care about how your business is operating. Though you may not have all the business savvy, each investor holds different standards of what they want to see in the startups they invest in. Some would like more maturity, while other would like less. Early stage investors don't care about growth as much as the problem being solved in an innovative way. Bringing your best and true self to the investment table despite flaws and lack of knowledge helps you weed out the investors who will and will not follow you for the long haul.

Chapter Ten: Market

Market

The most important part of any business model is creating a detailed description of your market, which includes identifying your customer, how can you reach them, and how you entice them to purchase your products and upsell them. This area requires the most research by the founder and their team.

Investors are interested in both the high level components and details of your market. This is where value and vision collide. Though you have a product or service, there needs to be a market for your product to turn your startup into a viable billion-dollar company.

How big is your target market or total addressable market (TAM)?

Market research is important before answering this question. This is going to lead you to what your customer segment looks like from a revenue perspective. There are statistics about most industries. If there's not, you can have companies and universities complete the research for you for a fee. If it's a university, they sometimes provide this service for free.

Experienced investors look for companies who have a Total Addressable Market (TAM) of at least twenty billion dollars. This is a guideline, not a rule to investing. Twenty billion is the magic number. The reason investor prefer the market to be twenty billion dollars is because if the company can obtain five percent market share (at a minimum), it stands to make ideal returns. For industries having a TAM of twenty billion dollars in revenue, they would produce at least one billion dollars in revenue if they have five percent market share. Founders with lower TAMs could still entice an investor with the potential growth opportunities of the company.

Who exactly is your target persona?

In almost every chapter customers have been addressed. Businesses must be customer-centric. Who is your customer? Be specific. Go back to your business model canvas and look at the customer segment. What does your customer do, how do they think, and what do they value? Check out these two examples as they relate to Business to Business (B2B) and Business to Consumer (B2C) target personas.

B2B Persona for an Adult Education Business

- Personal Name: Tim
- Age: 40-55
- Role: CIO and hiring manager
- Degree: Masters level
- Work Experience: 15 years of experience
- Focus: Empowering direct reports to work on their personal development
- Pain Points: Limited companies to work with in the area and not knowing what companies are credible. Retention caused

by the lack of the ability to distribute training across multiple locations.
- Fears: Hiring the wrong talent and have decreased employee retention, which would look bad as the leader.
- Pet Peeves: Lazy people.
- Hobbies: Traveling, Cooking, and Exercise.
- Internal Influences: HR Professionals, CEO, CFO, Board of Directors.
- Informational Sources: CIO Magazine, CIO Leadership Forum, Fast Business, Inc. Magazine, Forbes.

B2C Persona for a Social Media Business

- Persona Name: Renee Johnson
- Gender: Female
- Age: 35
- Relationship Status: Married
- Degree: Bachelor's degree or higher
- Homeowner: Yes
- Children: Yes
- Income: $80,000 - $100,000
- Location: East Coast United States
- Occupation: Small Business Owner
- Motivation: Being a successful entrepreneur and building an online brand while helping people
- Goals: Saving time, networking, share interesting content, and staying healthy.
- Where do they receive information: Internet (Social Media) and Mobile Apps.

Going through an entire persona can be longer than your actual pitch. As a founder pitching, be concise with your answer. Highlight the major important points of your customer; motivations, pain points, fears, and age for example.

How many locations and markets are you in?

This helps the investor know if your market strategy is to centralize or you disperse your operations across a state, region, or country. No answer is incorrect if you can validate the significance of your decision. Distribution isn't always about location. Virtual options and advanced shipping could subsidize costs of traditional logistics.

Where are you acquiring your market data?

This is important for the investor to verify the credibility of your information. If your data seems too good to be true, you will receive this question from a savvier investor. Believe it or not, founders have falsified market information to make their business more appealing to an investor. This investor understands where the most reliable data comes from. With ever-changing market conditions, it's wise to keep any statistical data about your market up to date. Your data can account for your own analysis of the market however making false claims can deter an investor from working with you. Understand why your data looks the way it does; how forecasts are trending and the best way to address any downturns or major changes in the market.

What type of conversations do you have with your target market?

Alternate Question: What do the customers within your target market and/or persona description say to you about your company?

Blindly creating a product or service without customer input is a big "No No." Investors want to know if you have reached out to your potential customer and asked what they want.

Have you received feedback on what your customer thought about your product, service, and your company? Focus on your persona and target market when receiving feedback.

What do you think your market will look like in three, five, or possibly ten years?

This can be a significant question as it relates to trends. As you look out ten years, predictions will become more bias and abstract due to changes in technology or demand. Your industry could go fully automated where in the current state there's little or no automation. A founder must be honest with the fact 5 years is the best they can do with foreseeing what their market will look like.

COVID-19 brought such a change into many markets in 2020. Industry segments such as home construction, e-learning, and home fitness had major increases in demand while brick and mortar restaurants and airline industries showed a significant decline. The pandemic shows how quickly industry trends can change.

What percentage of market share do you have?

Based on your market data, what percentage of the market do you have? If your target market contains a billion people and you have 100 million users or customers, then you have 10% of the market share. Most early stage startups have less than 0.001% of the market share when they look for investment. The goal for startups who have already received traction is to obtain approximately 1% - 5% within a year.

What percentage of the market share do you hope to obtain?

The obvious answer to this question is 100%, but it's just not realistic if you have competitors in your market. Not only must you answer realistically, but you must also answer based on short-term projections. If you don't, it's likely the follow-up question will be "How long will it take to reach this market share?"

Example: Let's use the previous example of one billion people and to-date owning ten percent of the market. If you have consistent exponential growth, you can calculate projected market share. Let's say your calculation over the next two years show projections of an additional fifty million users. Your response would be, "Based on my projections, we can secure five additional percent of the market over the next two years."

A rule of thumb is when you present these numbers (or any numbers) you are confident in how you came up with those figures.

What is your public relations (PR) strategy?

Within being customer-centric, communication is one of the key components of a startup. There's a consistent message you must present to your market. Remember brand engagement? PR keeps this trust flowing between the business and the company. Some businesses will live and die by the way they communicate which makes having a PR strategy important. Have a PR strategy for crisis too. Many things can go wrong in a startup and most new businesses are not prepared to address the issues or concerns to the public. Most large businesses are not prepared to address issues and concerns to the public either.

Example: In 2019, the famed airplane manufacturer, Boeing, lost all trust with its customers (the airlines) and many of its customers' customers (the travelers). Boeing didn't handle it well. Boeing, in the past known as the safest airline on the market, experienced two fatal crashes. Instead of adding a new safety system, they rejected the thought of installing it and worked to keep planes flying. Though Boeing worked to sweep all issues under the rug, external government investigators found a trail of negligence on Boeing's part. They put revenue over public safety, and it will diminish their reputation for a long time. With the right PR, Boeing could have mitigated the uncertainty, investigated the accident properly, and relayed mistakes in safety to the public and ways they will rectify the issues found.

What have you done for business continuity?

PR is only one piece of business continuity. I know from experience, planning for the unknown is vital to a business's continued operations. What if a computer server goes down, your CRM crashes and you lose all customer information, how do you stay operable if someone robs your business? What happens if your business catches fire? Business continuity makes sure you're prepared for any crisis.

Example: The COVID-19 pandemic is a prime example. It started in China in December 2019. While some companies were prepared for the disaster, other companies lost money, lost productivity hours, and lost traction. Companies laid off all their employees, global companies deployed billions of dollars in equipment for people to work at home and upgrade server capacity.

It's difficult to plan for the unknown, however there are business continuity and resilience companies who can provide not only an assessment but develop mitigation plans for your specific business. Being able to be lean and agile also helps if disaster hits your business. Your company can adapt by quickly making and executing on decisions.

What is your marketing strategy?

How you market your product or services goes back to the unique value proposition you provide and how it relates to your customer segment. Taking the information and packaging it into a message enticing people to buy is critical. You want people to purchase and to tell other people about your product. When was the last time you recommended a product or service to someone? Why did you do it? Good marketing supports your sales and branding, making your customers want to buy from you and refer other people.

What is your sales strategy?

If you haven't noticed yet, there's a different between PR, marketing, and sales. PR is what pushes people to think about your company. People want to buy from you because of your reputation and you build your reputation first through public relations. Marketing makes a person interested in buying what your company has to offer. Sales takes the person and makes them buy. All the strategies are important to create a business where people trust you and want to continue to buy from you.

Your sales strategy is another key component of the startup. More than anything, if you're not making sales, you're not running a viable business. Yes, you've pitched investors and sold them on your company. Selling your customer takes a fresh approach.

Why is this the right time for your product or service?

Geode or Google Pay?
CrunchPad or iPad?
Friendster or Facebook?
WebTV or Amazon Fire TV Stick?
Clinkle or Zelle?

Do you recognize these names? Probably the names on the right look familiar. The companies on the left provided the same product or service yet they launched too soon. Some with unfinished or clunky products and others before they were made ready to use. Having the right plan to develop and launch the product is key to the success of the business. Revolutionary products may be great, but not viable for the current market.

Are you sure you read the market correctly?

This is what the investor is thinking. This is also why it is so important for you to have done customer discovery prior to pitching your business. Launching a product or service is about having the right product/service at the right time for the right customer. If you launch too early, you will not obtain traction. If you launch too late, you've likely lost the market reach you planned to gain. Timing is everything, especially when you're working to launch something new.

Competition

Who are your competitors?

This question is important. Investors want to know who your competitors are, and if you realize who your competitors are. Knowing you have competitors directly or indirectly is vital from the standpoint of being a person with foresight. Just because a company doesn't do exactly what you do doesn't mean they are not a competitor.

Example: Blockbuster didn't view Netflix and Redbox as competition. Blockbuster owned over nine thousand video-rental stores in the United States. In 2010 Blockbuster filed for bankruptcy because it failed to keep up with competitors.

As mentioned earlier in the book, my first investors meetings happened at a soul-food restaurant with the founder. This man gave us a decent tour of his restaurant location as renovations just completed in his brick and mortar. The pitch he gave us was mediocre at best (in the eyes of a savvier investor now) but the answer to my question, "Who are your competitors?" became the most obvious reason I did not invest in him because he answered "NO ONE!" As I looked in the middle of the horseshoe-shaped strip mall, the first thing I notice; a Showmars, Burger King, Bar & Grill, Wendy's, Papa John's, Jersey Mike's, and Marco's Pizza. There were other restaurants nearby. His business sat two-and-a-half miles from a major interstate with even more restaurants between him and the interstate. Just because there were "no soul food restaurants around" (which Showmars sold their own version of soul food too), he didn't recognize competition. That was not the last time I heard someone say they had no competition.

When talking about your competition, it's better to go deep in your analysis versus being shallow about it? Analytical founders will find the smallest mom and pop shop and consider them competition if there's a slight chance their products or services align. You must create a competitor analysis in the middle, not too detailed and not too high level. No matter what, you will have competitors in your analysis.

Examples: Going back to the example of videos, look at Redbox. Once considered a revolutionary business, they contended with Blockbuster. Then streaming services came along and disrupted the industry even more. Those are the obvious competitors. Moreover, how do I increase my reach to beat my competitors? Redbox considered this, which is why placing their machines at the entrance of stores became a genius idea. Before you bought or thought about going to another location to rent your movie, you pass a Redbox machine and it will make you think twice before going to another location because of convenience.

Think about this competitor example. Cellphones are the most widely used technology devices during the time of writing this book. Cellphones to-date disrupt a major group of other technologies. It began with the home phone, pay phone (if you're old enough to remember those), then the pager. The cell phone now disrupts the computer and television market.

Why are you different from your competition?

In the case of the soul food restaurant, the difference between you and the competition can't only consist of being a soul food company. Setting your company apart from other competitors makes the difference. If you're a restaurant owner who serves a unique food, any other restaurant serving food (not necessarily "unique food") is a competitor. A business can set itself apart due to the story of the founder(s) or how they created the business. It could be an engaging brand like 19 Crimes Beer who uses an app and augmented reality to tell you a story of the person on one of their beer cans. This is where marketing and branding are important. Also, by taking your differentiators and placing them into your marketing, you create a memorable message to current and potential customers.

Examples: Airbnb does an amazing job at this. They've convinced travelers it's okay to stay in other people's homes versus staying at a local hotel when they travel. It's become so common to use Airbnb that their competitors (hotels) can be found on their website! They created a brand around their customers and the experience they receive when they travel. Many hotel brands didn't do that. The company is also big on social responsibility and displays it throughout their marketing platforms.

People know Ben and Jerry's for their social responsibility and transparency. Started by Ben Cohen and Jerry Greenfield, this ice cream company took the world by storm. There was a time on television it seemed an actor or actress could not eat ice cream unless it was Ben and Jerry's. Jerry believed, "If it's not fun, why do it?" Ben felt "Every company has a responsibility to give back to the community." Their brand displayed both ideologies. With new eccentric flavors being created constantly, it was fun to try the varieties. They led a plethora of initiatives to change the community. Ben and Jerry's believes in supporting our troops, multiple grant programs, environment justice, food sustainability, community development, and fair trade. They even own a foundation for philanthropic giving.

What are your strengths and advantages over your competitors?

Alternate Question: What is your competitive/unfair advantage?

Be honest with yourself and your potential investors concerning your strengths and weaknesses. A lot of incubators and accelerators teach how to complete SWOT analysis of your business.

Here are some examples of startup strengths:

- Size
- Ability to pivot
- Trademarks/Patents
- Have a product disruptor
- Great branding
- Superb customer service
- Large margins

You should create a SWOT analysis and design some of your strategy around it. Based on your strengths, weakness, opportunities, and threats, how are you improving your business? Presenting this to an investor makes them feel you have foresight into areas of improvement and the vision to execute change. Your strengths and weaknesses are areas of sustainability and incremental growth.

What are your weaknesses or disadvantages?

Weaknesses and disadvantages could be areas of growth or opportunity. When you're asked this question, don't be reluctant to tell the truth.

Here are some examples of startup weaknesses:

- Size
- Lack of funding
- High cost structure
- Gaps in team structure/capabilities

- Lack of access to industry support
- Saturated market
- Long sales cycles

Investors want to hear and deserve to hear the truth. Weaknesses and disadvantages can also double as an advantage and disadvantage. A magnificent example of a disadvantage and an advantage is company size. It could be a disadvantage being a small company because other businesses do not take you seriously, but the advantage of your size could be your ability to reduce your pricing, be more flexible because you have less overhead, and have a culture of agility. On the other side of pricing, being small could make your costs and prices higher. You may not have the volume to decrease your prices until you obtain traction.

What barriers to entry or scale are there for you?

Barrier to entry coincide with the "threats" section of your SWOT analysis.

Here are some examples of barriers to entry or scale:

- Government Laws and regulations
- Cost
- Technology
- Distribution/Logistics
- Being an unknown player in the industry

Laws and regulations are the biggest barriers to entry or scale. During this period, the cannabis industry is booming, but many people cannot enter this industry because of the laws and regulations written by each state. Complying with these laws and regulations also come with a heavy price tag for a founder looking to join the industry. Others are fearful because there are strong federal laws still making some types of cannabis illegal to grow, sell, or use.

The coronavirus became a barrier to entry for companies who wanted to open brick and mortar stores. Mentees of mine wanted to start a store in an airport and looked to sign a lease as the pandemic took place. The orders of many states to stay-at-home placed their dreams on pause. They haven't opened the store, and it forced the entrepreneurs to think differently about their strategy.

How have you mitigated this(these) risk(s)?

The barriers to entry and the company's weaknesses and disadvantages are all risks which can lead to failure if not properly addressed. How would a founder mitigate the risks or use them to their advantage? Are you working with legislators to change the laws and regulations? Are you looking for more money to combat cost issues? Have you tapped into your network to fix distribution/logistical problems? Are their experts on your team who can bring your cost down and make you a bigger competitor into the market? There are always solutions to mitigate risks. Some solutions take longer than others, yet they're still solutions.

How do you make your company more scalable?

Investors expect their founders to show vision and influence in their company and industry. The ability to stay relevant and scale your business is one of the most important jobs of a CEO. Founders must put together a long-term roadmap to implement and enhance their products or services. Scaling isn't always about new customers, it's also about expanding revenue opportunities. You can also do this through developing or enhancing features needed to upsell or cross sell a current customer. Retention is important because those who received a pleasurable experience with your service will come back again and stay a customer.

Where is the competition letting down customers?

Your competition may not be the biggest concern as a startup, but as founders scale, customers' feelings about their competitors makes a difference. Study your competition. Look at the history of Wendy's Twitter page and how they "roast" their competitors because of their mediocre food. Many other companies have targeted the faults of their competitors for their own gain. It can be a good marketing strategy.

Why haven't your competitors done this yet?

If your product or service is so exceptional and unique, why hasn't your competitor tried it? If you say your idea is unique, an investor will often ask the questions to verify this is a viable and outstanding idea. As an investor, follow-up with other companies to understand why they haven't implemented a product one of their potential founders planned to launch. Don't give away too much. There are a lot of copycats out there, but it allows the investor to receive another company's perspective on the industry.

How do your features differ?

If you completed your business model canvas, you probably have a solid value proposition. Most likely part of your value proposition includes the feature or features making you different in the industry. Benchmarking and general comparisons help realize where you stand out from the crowd. Too often, investors hear, "no one else is doing this" when there are several companies who are. Your own due diligence makes your strategy of marketing and product development easier.

How do you compare on price?

Once again, benchmarking and price comparisons are very helpful in a startup. Even if there are companies who do only part of what you do, it's great to meet founders who have really done their homework and have been thoughtful in how they price their products or services.

How do you compare on service?

This investor will challenge you to try one or more of your competitors' products or services as not just a benchmark but a way to obtain the experience as a customer. Before being asked, do it yourself. Invest the money to try a competitor's product or service, understanding their process and how it compares to yours.

How do you compare on customer satisfaction?

Though your service may be great, how does the customer feel about it? This goes back to benchmarking or having someone benchmark for you. Use company reviews to understand what customers are saying and, if possible, interview people who have purchased a similar product or service. You owe it to your business to have some understanding of what your competitors are doing. It will help you stand out amongst the crowds.

Understanding your market helps create a product and service worthy of an investment. Your market helps understand the who, where, and why of your business while your product is the "what." Complete your market research, understand how the customer feels, and use the talents of sales and marketing to create revenue for your business.

Chapter Eleven: Legal

Legal and Corporate Structure

Legal matters are sensitive to startups. Though many founders start with bootstrapping and use boilerplate legal documents (and other documents) to create their businesses, they will need legitimate legal advice as the startup expands. Change is constant in the legal world so it's important for both the founder and their legal counsel to be current on the newest changes in the laws.

A solid legal foundation is essential for a business. The team must be in place, the startup needs structure, and they must sign all agreements. More documents will ensue as you grow. Have a legal team review documents before signing, especially when it involves capital investments.

How is the business structured?

Corporate structure is important but not always necessary to structure correctly the first time. Your company will develop, and your needs will change as your business grows. During the formation of your business, you will choose what type of corporation you need. Many investors investing based your legal structure and your line of business, understand the state and federal laws related to the structure you choose. Founders or their legal team must keep up with the ever-changing tax laws related to their business structure as well.

Who holds which titles?

If there are multiple founders, you cannot have all of them as the CEO. For you and your founding team to understand their roles and responsibilities, you must develop them. Once agreed upon, the founders should sign an operating agreement stating their roles and responsibilities. Investors know one of the key mistakes novice businesses make, (especially with multiple founders) is not laying out roles and responsibilities. It can cause confusion, chaos, and decreased productivity. Worst case, it will break the founders apart and end the startup.

How are shares split?

Most founders don't give employees shares in the business early in the game because there are usually not shares established yet. You may receive this question more with co-founders and founders who have done equity raises. Stock shares mean little when there's little or no growth. The company's bylaws however should state how many shares they allow the business to distribute. This creates a guideline as the business continues to grow.

Can you provide documents to verify stock ownership?

This is a legal document investors want to make sure is correct. If there are more stocks owned than agreed upon, these documents should reflect an accurate amount. Companies often purchase "corporate kits" for around a hundred dollars to set up their corporation legally with stock certificates. It's a good starting point for any business. The corporate kit normally includes a company seal, stock certificates, a board meeting minutes book, and a transfer ledger. Kits vary based on customization.

Is there an existing board or advisors?

Most investors want to be on the board to make company decisions. It's important to have a board or advisors keen on who you are, your goals, and to speed up your business growth. Big investors expect to be part of the board of directors. This board is your guiding team for growth and prosperity.

Follow-up Questions:

- If yes, what is their experience?
- If yes, can I meet them all?
- If no, why have you not created a board?

Where is the business registered?

You will usually hear this from the investor or their lawyer to determine what the structure is and what it might look like. As stated earlier, investors are partial to the startup friendly state of Delaware. When developing your structure, no matter where you register, you will still need to keep up with the state laws of the registration state.

Who handles your accounting?

Hire an accountant! Most startup founders do not possess this knowledge and doing it yourself could be extremely detrimental to your business in the long run. You should hire an accountant experienced with working with businesses. Certified Public Accountants (CPAs) are licensed accountants who have a fiduciary responsibility to your business to make sure you make decisions in the best interest of the company. Also different from a regular accountant, CPAs follow a strict code of ethics and come with a higher level of standards.

Good accounting and bookkeeping a basic part of preparing for due diligence. Having a central location to put your financials is key because the organization's financial documentation will be a sizeable piece of what the investors want to see. For a startup, there are some great free options to an accounting platform with people who will help your basic tax needs. It's also great to have an accountant who can support you through the tax process. You want trusted accountants savvy with working knowledge of business taxes and accounting.

What unique skills and talents do each founder/key person contribute?

No owner or founder is a holistic businessperson. They may understand a lot about business, but all founders and key people have their own unique core competencies to make their business effective. If their major strength does not negatively affect the company in their absence, then they are not a key person in your business.

Who filed the business? Who is the registered agent on record?

Sometimes a company has a non-founder file for the corporation and EIN for them. If an investor is digging into your paperwork, and the name of the person who filed your paperwork is unfamiliar, they may want to know who and why they completed the paperwork for you. Many times, it's a consultant or lawyer but the founder can easily file the paperwork themselves.

Do you have any standing agreements with other parties?

Investors, suppliers, vendors, old co-founders can all be people who you have a current agreement. Disclose the agreements because they may make a difference in your valuation. Also, investors have a relationship with other suppliers and vendors who might provide the same products or services at a discounted rate. I have known investors to renegotiate poorly written agreements in a way to improve the bottom line.

Intellectual Property

What is unique about the business?

This is specific to your business. It answers the question of why someone would buy from you versus a competitor. What product, service, or experience does your customer receive other companies do not provide. Even more important, is it proprietary? Do you have anything to prove it is proprietary?

What legal risks do you see?

To answer this question, you must know the problem and how your consumers or potential consumers feel about this problem. Are their any risks if your product or service doesn't work and you could be sued? Your answer represents the awareness you have around your business. In an era where any individual can sue a company at any moment, there's always some kind of legal risk involved in running a business. Mainly financial, healthcare, and software businesses receive this question. There's large liability in handling someone's money. There's also liability and tons of compliance around financial and healthcare industries.

In a world of big data, one of the most talked about risks is around privacy, data, facial recognition, and information sharing. If you're running a technology startup, it's critical you have all your ducks in a row. How are you securing your data and preventing others from accessing it? Some companies sell their data. Are you stating it in your privacy policy and is the user acknowledging it's okay to sell them?

Are you aware of any product liability risks?

Product-based businesses may have recalls, breaks, and electrical issues causing the user to become injured. When designing your product, think of all the concerns. Could batteries blow up, could someone become trapped in your product, or could manufacturing mistakes harm your customers? If it can happen to major companies, it can happen to your startup. This is a good area to also collaborate with your PR and business continuity partners on.

Examples: Think of the recall of Tylenol in the 80s, the salmonella in peanut butter, faulty Takata airbags, defective Samsung batteries, or even poorly manufactured Firestone tires. These types of product issues can send a startup out of business quickly. The mistakes cost these companies anywhere between $100 million to $24 billion dollars. This doesn't include the loss of future business from consumers.

What regulatory risks could affect this business?

Laws and regulatory risks can shut down a company. A founder new to the industry often overlooks this. It's easy to do when you're worried about running a fast-growing company. I've found many founders having advisors in the industries which they are unfamiliar. When you're in areas requiring a lot of compliance and regulatory requirements, you want to have someone on your team who can advise on these issues. Bring in a lawyer.

What intellectual property do you own?

Trademarks, patents, copyrights, and trade secrets are what can help you stand apart from your competitors. Investors feel differently patents. Some think they're a great opportunity to give you runway to grow while others think it's a waste of time or a scam. Intellectual property also includes trade secrets preventing companies from duplicating what makes you successful. We also know trade secrets as proprietary information.

Examples: Kentucky Fried Chicken, Coca Cola, McDonald's, and Krispy Kreme all have secret recipes "locked in a safe" at their company headquarters. Trade secrets go beyond food recipes. WD-40's formula for their rust preventing spray is a trade secret. Companies choose trade secrets instead of patents because once submitted to the United States Patent and Trademark Office (USPTO), patents become public record. Trade Secrets ensures only a select group of trusted company associates possess the secret.

Companies also define their processes as trade secrets. The most elusive process in the publishing world is how to become designated as a New York Times Bestseller. Unlike the name sounds, it's believed there's more to this list than selling a lot of books. The New York Times refuses to confirm or deny the allegations.

Who developed any intellectual property owned?

Did you develop the patented work? Did you design the trademarked work? Did you write the copyrighted manuscript? If someone outside of the founder developed a patent, trademark, or copyright they are likely the owners unless you have showed otherwise in an agreement. It's customary to include any work being done on company time or company property to be part of the company, not the individual who creates it. This must be part of your employee agreement however.

Have any employees or partners who left the company able to challenge these rights?

If you own this intellectual property, can or will someone challenge your right to own the intellectual property? Yes, people challenge ownership to intellectual property. If you have the right agreements in place, you shouldn't have to worry about this.

Has the USPTO awarded any patents?

The patent process is lengthy and about 52% become awarded. This shouldn't discourage any founder from wanting to file for patents. Patents are not the end all for startups. Elon Musk patented Tesla technology to develop electric cars, then released the patents so other developers and carmakers had a blueprint to develop their own. In his effort to support environmental sustainability and fight climate change, Musk felt it would speed up this agenda.

Are there any additional patents pending or planned?

Pending patents gauges uniqueness and can increase the valuation of your company. Planned patents could also let the investor know you may have a greater foothold in the marketplace because of the patent.

How are any current intellectual assets owned?

Is the intellectual asset owned by you, the founder, or your company? Intellectual property can be included in the valuation of a business and if any part of your business is divested, this answer matters. Investors must make the determination if intellectual property makes the business unique and is a contributing factor in the company making money.

Having your legal information in order helps the business continue to run smoothly. Poor legal representation, contracts or agreements can stop a thriving startup in a matter of minutes. It's important to have documents completed, detailed where necessary, and organized for easy reference.

Chapter Twelve: Financials

Financials

The most successful founders know their numbers inside and out. You don't need a degree in finance, only an understanding of the numbers related to your business and why they're important. A financial team can do all the calculations for you. It's your job to know and understand the results.

While interviewing investor, Brandon Banner, he told me about his view on working with startups and small businesses. "It's amazing to me and this is what I find out about business owners. Most business owners don't know the answers [about their financials and processes]. They're good at what they do and not business. [Using a landscaper as an example] They can cut your grass well, but if I ask how much they spend on gas or what is their biggest expense, they don't know the amount. The business processes are mainly why the company needs an investor's help. The P&L, the liabilities and expenses, how much money did you make and send out? You can cut the hell out of grass, but you're not thinking how to lower expenses and people cost."

In the following questions, we'll talk about the numbers and which are important to your potential investors. Of all these questions, the fundamental question will always go back to "How will

I get my money back?" and "When will I get my money back?" Banner mentioned, "If I give you a dollar, how am I going to get $1.25 back?"

How much of your own money did you put into this business?

There are two reasons this question may come up. The investor wants to know if the founder(s) invested their money into the business. This can be very important to understand the buy-in the founder has into their business. The investor also wants to know if the founder believes in their business. If the founder is not willing to invest his or her own money into the business, what does it say about how much the founder believes it will work?

How much are you raising?

This is a simple question. Knowing how much the raise is can provide an investor with an idea of how many investors there may be, or the investors needed to close the round. It will also help gauge the amount of money they might need in the future. Often a founder will over or underestimate their valuation. It's up to the investor to understand how much runway the current raise will offer the founder (reference their burn rate) and the possibility they'll need more money. This will allow the investor to structure their deal with the founder accordingly.

How can you still scale your business with less capital?

An investor will ask this question for a few reasons. First, they believe the founder can execute growth with less capital. There's no benefit in the company losing equity on a large raise when they can grow for less funding.

It's not beneficial to the founder or investor. To oversubscribe your round is not always the best for a business either. Founders with too much money tend to eat into their acquired capital faster. They have no regard for spending less and being conservative. Being conservative in their spending could help founders grow faster, slow the period to do another round of investing, and let them possess a reserve of money to absorb any unforeseen issues.

Second, the investors are challenging the founder to think leaner in the way they do business. This could be a major learning moment for a founder, and it could help them slow the bleeding of money. Even if they continue to raise the same amount of funding dollars, they save money to scale faster.

Third, investors can secure a sizable piece of the pie with a small capital raise. If the founder drops their raise amount, the investor may acquire more equity gain in the business. It's important for the founder to know how much they need and why they need it. An investor should not be able to make a founder who's done the proper evaluation of their own business drop their capital raise significantly.

How much is your marketing budget?

As a part of every financial strategy, it's important to create a budget. How much do you plan to spend on marketing, advertising, and branding to reach your sales goals? If you want to be fancy, a pro forma will cover all financials, including marketing. There's no magic number on how much you must spend. You can determine this as you identify your target customer and create your entire budget.

What are your per customer acquisition costs (CAC)?

The cost to obtain a customer varies based on marketing, your product and your industry. It's important the CAC is not equal or more than your customer's lifetime value (LTV).

How soon do you recover the CAC?

If you send out one hundred mailers and on average receive one customer a month from the time they receive the mailers, this is your CAC recovery time. Long recovery times reduce cash flow and can be a pain point for investor unless your product is a high dollar item (like a Prada purse or Bentley car).

How much is your customers' lifetime value (LTV)?

The LTV of the customer is important. If the customers purchase top dollar products or if they repeatedly buy the product, it's important to know how much revenue a customer will spend during your relationship with them. As part of tracking sales, you can show how many times a customer repurchases. It's easier for some products versus others.

Example: An individual will purchase approximately three homes in their lifetime, on average. Depending on their socioeconomic status, the average changes. As a realtor, my average home sell may be $250,000. If each client bought three homes, the LTV of a customer would be $750,000.

A Software-As-A-Service (SaaS) company with many a la carte features may consume an arduous amount of time properly calculating LTV unless they've been in business for a long time. LTV may also be tiered or segmented by the type of product or service you provide and/or by the customer type.

How much equity and debt have you accumulated in the past?

Alternate Question: What stock options have you given already?
Alternate Question: What is the distribution of equity between founders?

An investor wants to hear the words "none" if they're really interested in your product. I say this jokingly and not so jokingly. If other investors possess equity, potential investors favor the founders still holding on to the majority stake in their business. With debt, it's important an investor knows you're using your personal and business credit wisely. Poor management of debt or vast accumulation of debt can cause a potential investor to pull out of a seemingly great deal.

How much debt do you own now?

Debt is important to an investor. Having some debt is not an enormous deal, but to have major debt as a startup may reveal red flags. Acquiring debt happens when there are capital expenses or a need to possess money quickly to keep your business's momentum going. Using debt to acquire office space or a "business vehicle" when you've work effectively from home or you possess little need to travel for your business is unreasonable to an investor. Debt is also a factor in how the deal is structured. It's in the founder's best interest to only accumulate debt when absolutely necessary.

What is your burn rate?

It's no doubt growing startups spend money quickly. Based on growth and the right systems, it's simple to monitor and forecast monthly spend. This is called your burn rate. How much money are you burning (spending) monthly? There's a need to hire employees, upgrade technology, and sometimes rent office space scalable to your needs and the spend related to those expenses but be accounted for.

What is your upside?

Investor are always looking to gauge the value and increase the value of your company. Your upside is the potential increase in value whether monetary or market reach.

Do you rent commercial real estate?

Specifics of large expenses such as commercial real estate are a major part of finances. Some investors have the ability or connections to help you receive a lower lease amount which will save your company money. There are also negotiation consultants who do the same.

How much does it cost to rent office space in your city?

There are two reasons an investor wants to know this. First, they want to know how other office spaces compare to the location you're renting. Second, the investor wants to know you were thoughtful in your office space decision. Choosing an office space usually comes down to convenience (for either the founders or their customer) and/or price. Some founders who have a lot of face-to-face client interaction are also looking for a space representing the quality of their brand.

Are you cash-flow positive?

A business being cash flow positive means an investor has an increased chance of receiving their money back. It also shows the startup has some runway to cover additional expenses, even if they're small. At the earliest stages of a revenue generating startup, smart founders put profits back into the business anyway and this can be a moot point.

How long will it take to become profitable?

Again, an investor is interested in when they'll receive a return. If you are not already making a profit, the investor is thinking how the startup can make profits quickly, receive a return, and estimate future returns.

What are the key metrics your team focuses on?

It's important for a founder to know their numbers. Though they may bring on a CFO, having a founder who doesn't know the numbers means they can't properly make strategic decisions for the business. Investors do not limit metrics to your financials, but what makes your business thrive? Ask yourself, what are the key people, processes, and tools important for you to make business decisions. If you can decide without a process or tool, it's likely not a key metric.

Example: Founder, Latonia Miller has been growing her medical practice for over five years. Being a business owner, she understood the balance sheets and the profit and loss statements, but it wasn't until she started digging deeper did her numbers change.

She realized sixty-three percent of her clients came in three to four times a year. Her growth was extremely slow, though the company was sustaining itself. Miller could look at the demographic of her current clients and create a marketing strategy around the population of people like the clients she was already serving.

She also realized her profit margins month over month looked like a roller coaster with a five percent drop in the middle of the year. She realized her margins declined dramatically because one supplier increased their prices and her cost varied based on the number of supplies she purchased. Latonia adjusted her purchasing schedule and found another supplier to replace the one who increased their prices which raised her profit margins higher than ever.

[For B2B companies] What's your annual contract value (ACV)?

Small businesses and startups look to grab business and government contracts to provide large enough revenue to gain traction, hand over less equity, and provide bigger and better numbers to investors. Most contracts last six months to a year. If it's a government contract, they can go beyond three years.

Do you have any sales?

Don't be ashamed to say "No." If there's no sales, there's an explanation why. If you possess sales, let the investor know your sales and your end-of-year projections.

What are your sales-to-date?

Profit it not always the best sign of growth. As a company grows, they incur more expenses. Sales determines the demand for the product and how well the sales and marketing strategy is going. Sales-to-date allows a potential investor to compare your growth over months, quarters, or years. If an investor knows how long you've been in business, which they don't when they first meet you, they want to develop a rough estimate of what the expected revenue will be over a certain period.

What have you sold this year?

I've met founders who made over $100,000 in overall sales-to-date, but it accounted for about ten years of sales. Investors are interested in what's happening now and not ten years ago. Comparing sales-to-date to current year sales helps an investor know the traction you've gained from the time you began selling to now. It puts a lot of perspective on the growth of the company.

How many purchases does your average customer make?

This question relates to the lifetime value (LTV) of a customer mentioned earlier in this chapter. Is your product or service a one-purchase item or will the customers need to buy periodically?

Example: Considering household items such as toothpaste, the average person buys 7.6 regular sized tubes a year. This means for Crest who has loyal customers, they can expect their customers to make approximately 7-8 purchases each year per each family member in their household.

Where do most of your sales come from?

"Where" includes your location, product, and customer. If asked, let the investor know what product is selling the most, what type of customer is purchasing the most, and what location those customers are coming from.

Example: When listening to a pitch of a local business in Charlotte, NC they informed me most of their business came from online sells of their custom-made products though they owned a collection of pre-made products. They also let us know most of their sales came from women who lived in Virginia who were buying the products as a gift for the men in their lives (mostly husbands).

They acquired this information through their ecommerce site by asking their sex, and if the item was a gift or not. Men were the target for the custom product they already made, so it wasn't difficult to figure out these were gifted to men. They included the billing and shipping addresses in the online payment, so it became easy to figure out the demographic of the seller and user.

How will you sell the product?

There're many ways to sell a product. Primarily you will sell online and/or in some physical/retail location. In retail, you could rent a kiosk in the mall or a booth at the local farmers' market, a trade show, or pop-up shop. As pop-up shops are becoming popular, other ways to sell a product is through mobile stores. Service companies began providing mobile services decades ago, however only within the last decade have mobile stores become the trend for product-based businesses. This includes food trucks, mobile coffee shops, mobile cigar bars, bookstore, etc. Businesses are using this strategy to reach more customers in different locations with less overhead.

Will the company be able to sell in five to seven years?

Three years of financial projections are enough to provide an investor. Five to seven years is a stretch and could create a false narrative of what your business can do financially. The investor's interest though is if the company will grow to a point in the five to seven-year period in which it will go IPO or be large enough to be acquired by another company.

Existing Financing Round

Going into the round, you the founder must know:

- The amount of money you need
- What you will use the money for
- The value of your company

- How much equity you're willing to hand over

It's important you do not let go of too much equity when you first raise because you may end up losing the controlling stake in the company before making it to the next round.

What is your exit goal? (i.e. IPO, M&A)

Investors make the most money upon exiting the business. They want to know if you've even thought about exiting your company. Startups with traction and a good foothold on customers are always being scouted by larger or complimentary businesses to acquire. Many founders are looking to reach IPO and stay on as the CEO of the company. Not to say this is a pipe dream, but going IPO seldom happens in the startup world.

Who do you imagine will help you exit?

This involves a team to help you exit your company. From the support of your founders and lawyers (maybe even a psychologist), you will need a team to support the transition with you. Though this is not asked normally of startups, it's good to know if a founder is thinking about this.

What's the minimum price you would exit for?

If being acquired or purchased is your goal, keep in the back of your mind the value of the company and how much you would sell it for. Knowing the range in which you would sell your business at any unexpected moment is vital. For some founders, it helps them work toward a valuation goal.

Has anyone else offered money?

Believe it or not, founders turn down money. It could be for the reason of not needing money at the time or not feeling the investor is right fit for the company.

How much did you raise in your friends and family round?

Some founders start with a friend and family rounds however it's not mandatory. Friend and family rounds solidify how much those closest to you believe in you and your startup idea.

How much equity are you giving up?

As angel investor Brandon Banner says, "Money pays an investors way in. They don't have to provide knowledge, resources, and connections. Advice comes at a price." It's important for the founder to know the value of the business, but it's also important to know the value of the potential investor. Investors want to help your business grow, but with a large portfolio of businesses, "time is money" (shout out to my brother Andrae who lives by this slogan).

What round of funding are you in?

Funding rounds are periods in which a startup works to raise a set amount of money. A round may start with pre-seed funding also known as the friends, family, and fools (FFF) round. The official funding round goes through the alphabet (series A, series B, series C, etc.). The earlier the round, the riskier the investment.

How much are you trying to raise now?

Alternate Question: *What is the size of the round and will the injection be worth the return?*

A founder shouldn't just go to investors with no idea of how they are valuing the company. They shouldn't go in not understanding how much they want to raise in this round. Does the valuation make sense to the investor? There are several ways in which a founder values their business.

Each funding round has a set dollar amount the company is looking to raise at a set valuation. An under subscribed round is one where the founder did not meet their dollar goal. An oversubscribed round is when the founder surpassed their goal, because they still left the round open for more funding.

Would you lower your market cap for a larger amount of funding?

Your market cap is the total value of your company. If you lower your market cap for more money, the investor would receive more equity in your business.

What is your expected time frame for this round?

Founders can create an estimated deadline to complete their rounds based on growth, and to keep business momentum going. Starting out, it takes less time but more effort to raise funds. Founders expect to participate in raising between twelve to eighteen months per round with a six to twelve month break in between. In later rounds, a founder expects closer to eighteen months or more time spent raising capital.

Who took part in earlier rounds of fundraising?

This is the time to name drop if you maintain well-known angels and VCs who invested in your company. Funders with high reputations entice other angels to inject capital, especially if the funder injected multiple rounds.

How many previous investors will take part in this round?

This is a similar question and respond in the same way. Name drop as much as possible because it will build your business credibility. If you sell a fitness product and one of your investors is a Super Bowl champion or Wimbledon Cup winner, you hold more clout to any interested investors.

How will you use this round of financing to grow your business?

Capital raises should not be used to create a rainy-day fund, it's for the purpose of building the business. If you owned a widget company and you're losing money due to lack of sales and marketing, your key goal may be to build a sales and marketing team. Many founders use the money for research and development, expanding production, or expanding to other locations.

Based on the information you've told the investor already, they've considered how they think you must spend your funds. They want to make sure you agree, and you've thoughtfully considered how to use the funds to grow.

What is the next milestone this money will take you to?

Though there is a goal, or multiple goals, to every round, there are milestones within each goal. Using the previous widget company who wants to increase sales and marketing, there will be milestone to building a sales and marketing team. You could hire a consultant to complete a strategic analysis and execution plan. Hiring a fractional Chief Marketing Officer (CMO) may be another marketing milestone. "Fractional" means a part-time consultant who has significant experience in a certain area whether it be marketing, finance, sale, operations, etc. Brand building or hiring a team may be other milestone to complete your funding goal.

When do you expect you will conduct a follow-up round of fundraising?

Fundraising is a full-time job. It takes a lot from the founder and they still need to run a booming business. Each funding round helps provide about a year of financial runway to keep the business going. This provides the founder six to twelve months to focus on the direction of the business before starting their next funding round.

How much is your pre-money valuation?

When a company has not produced revenue, they can still raise funds. Whether they've gained traction does not matter. If it's an innovative idea, they will still draw investor interest. A pre-money valuation is the value you're putting on your company before it brings in revenue. If you're benchmarking your valuation off another business or not, here's how you can calculate this.

Valuation = amount of funding asked for / percent of equity to be given

Amount of funding asked for = Valuation x Percent of equity to be given

Percent of equity to be given = Amount of funding asked for / Valuation

How are you determining current valuation?

There's no silver bullet to figure out the value of your company. Some founders hire experts, others price compare with similar companies. There are other methods depending on the product and company growth. The founder may not come up with the value, however they must understand how they determined the calculation.

Valuation for startups begin with benchmarking valuations with similar companies. For companies who have received funding, the SEC provide benchmark information through their EDGAR database and through investor.com. This will give you an idea of the size of the company and what they have valuated their business at. Experienced business brokers have expertise in looking at industries and creating a valuation. Hiring a broker to do this for you can be an option.

Benchmarking techniques can also focus on market potential. Comparing the reach of other companies have who sell similar products and services helps gauge who the customers are, how much they're willing to pay, and if there's something unique about the startups that caters to the potential market. When you do not have revenue yet, researching the market potential is important.

Revenue is another way to valuate a business. Usually a startup will take their revenue and increase that number by a specific multiple. Using a price-to-earnings ratio and multiplying it by the projected earnings. If the price-to-earnings ratio for a company like yours is 10 and your project your earnings to be $300,000 a year, then your business would be worth $3 million.

Evaluating growth is useful to valuate your business when you have a freemium model with future aspirations to have paid features into your platform. By looking at user growth a company can estimate the value of converting freemium customers into paying customers.

Are you including projected sales into your valuation?

When using company growth to evaluate your company, they include sales, however projected sales can either strengthen an investor's view on the company or not. Projections are only estimations and if your current sales are unstable, an investor will lean towards a lower valuation.

Would you consider being bought out? If so, how much?

The valuation and the purchase price are two different amounts. If an investor tries to buy you out, they will not necessarily look to do it at the valuation price. Buyouts involve higher numbers, maybe even a term in which the founder stays with the company and helps it grow. Buyouts could also provide the founder with an equity stake and/or a salary in the company.

Why do you think your business is worth it?

Lay on the story, the passion, and how your business affects your customers. Talk about the sales, growth, and the testimonials of those who purchased from your company. The worth of a company isn't always in the sales when starting off. The influence your product or service makes is just as valuable.

How soon can I (as the investor) receive my money?

Alternate Question: How do I receive my money back and when?

No founder or investor can predict when the return of the dividends will be after payment. Startups are ever-changing, and predicting this can only come from looking through the financials. More experienced founders can estimate their returns based on current traction. If they do not believe they'll receive their money back, with interest, within three to seven years, it's likely they will not invest. Family Offices tend to stay around for a longer term and may not mind the delayed returns. Those instances where it's hard to understand when the returns will come, an investor will probably opt for a non-equity deal.

Example: Instead of taking twenty-five percent of your business, the investor will take a two-dollar royalty payment from every item sold until the founder returns their money, then drop the price to one dollar in perpetuity (meaning forever or until an undetermined date).

Would you prefer to do a royalty deal or equity deal?

To prevent giving up equity in your business, you may opt for a royalty deal. Once again, it's a decision you as a founder must consider before walking into a pitch room or starting due diligence. There are pros and cons to doing each, but what is best for your startup?

Why do you want me (as the investor) to invest in your business besides providing capital?

Alternate Question: Why would I be your ideal investor?
Alternate Question: Do you want a partner or just the investment of money?
Alternate Question: How else do you hope an investor will help beyond money?

The answer to this question shows you've done your own research on the investor or firm. There's a level of responsibility a founder ought to take in knowing the value of the investor. When many startups go on *Shark Tank*, they think of the value of the investors and the value of being on the show. Through this, they make an informed decision on the "sweat equity" value of each investor outside of the monetary value they will provide.

Investors do the same. They evaluate their own worth and come to the table ready to negotiate the valuation based on what they bring to the table, whether it be working in your business, connections, or knowledge of the industry you don't possess.

Why would you want to give away part of your business?

Some companies are premature in their search for funds. When deciding to raise, there's a level of analysis you need to do in your company. Timing is important and some investors who think you didn't exhaust all options, or you do not need the funding, will not bother with giving you money.

Use of Funds

Are you looking to a loan/debt or to give up an equity stake in your business?

It's important for founders to come into due diligence understanding the advantages and disadvantages of taking debt over equity.

Advantages of a loan/debt versus equity

- You can write off the interest of the loan on your taxes.
- The terms of engagement are simple. I provide you money and you pay me back with a certain interest rate and payment schedule.
- The founder keeps their equity stake in the startup.
- You don't need to give up a board seat.
- Periodic reporting isn't necessary to provide the lender.

Disadvantages of a loan/debt versus equity

- You must pay the money back in full, with interest, or it will affect your business credit.
- If not paid back, you could lose collateral used to apply for the loan, like a house or car.
- The requirements to receive funding can be a lot more stringent. There's a certain debt-equity ratio and cash flow needed to qualify.
- Interest rate could be high and create greater pressure to make money quickly, which could create poor decision-making opportunities.
- It will take increased financial awareness and budgeting to make sure you submit payments as agreed upon.

How can you push the price down on the amount of money you want?

Investors are always thinking of how to increase margins and cater to the affordability need of the target customer. Bringing the price down by improving internal processes, changing materials, and changing the product features will help the buying decisions process easier.

How much will you spend on founders' salaries?

If your startup is at the seed stage, paying the founders is not always an expectation. A business making no or little profit is using their money to put back into the business just to get traction.

How much will you spend on overhead versus expansion?

Though a founder may know their numbers, predicting expansion cost is vital. Many times, founders expect expansion of employees but do not account for rent, utilities, or human resource costs.

What if you don't receive all the money you are asking for?

Alternate Question: Could funding stop the business from ceasing to operate?
What is your plan B? If you do not receive capital, will you continue to bootstrap or will your startup cease to exist? This shows two things; your ability to be lean, keep your business going, and the sense of urgency the founder has to make a deal work. If you respond to this indicating your business will still exist and you have a plan, that's great. If the investor believes your business will no longer exist, they may make a deal more pleasing to them or wait until more investors agree to invest first. For the founder, there are other investors out there. You can always keep pushing for funds elsewhere. The pool of available money should not run dry for you.

What assets will be invested in with this capital?

Similar to a previous question, what are you going to do with my money? More specifically, what assets are you going to purchase and why do you think it will speed up the business? The investor is expecting returns from their money, not for you to tell them you will put it in business equipment that looks nice but creates no value.

What are your milestones?

Investors can base their funding from milestones created by the founder. To avoid a higher burn rate, you could receive equity payments incrementally based on the startup's growth roadmap.

What are the biggest risks to my investment?

Investors will not likely ask this question directly however this is what they want to know. Though all investments hold risk and startups being some of the riskiest, an investor want to gauge the risk level. Through most of the other questions in this book, they will gauge their level of risk to invest. The level depends on the customer segment, industry, founder, team, and product/service being provided to a customer.

Why are you choosing this method of raising capital?

Not all startups need to raise capital through equity. An investor may want to know you've thought through all options to obtain funds for your business.

How much of this money will be used for future fundraising efforts?

There are costs involved in raising capital. There's travel, products, due diligence expenses, etc. Though you may not think so, some investment capital goes into future fundraising efforts.

How much are your personal expenses each month?

Some founders struggle to separate personal and business expenses. I can't tell you how many times I've spoken with founders who use their business profits to pay their non-business bills. If an investor feels you use money to pay for your personal expenses, they will probably not invest in your business unless they're positive you will change this habit. Receiving a loan or line of credit may be a better option for you to receive capital.

This is the largest chapter of the book because it's one of the most important to an investor. There are many unknowns in business but when there are ways to project success based on quantitative information, investors jump at the opportunity to know more. It's not just about a good idea, it's about a good idea that's workable and has great growth potential.

Chapter Thirteen: Product or Service Specific

Product Specific

How long has your product been on the market?

This is important for three reasons. The time your product has been on the market compared to company traction is a sign of failure or success. Often on *Shark Tank* you'll find a founder who's had their product on the market for eight years, however they've only made one thousand dollars. Timing is important when launching a product. If the product hits the market at the right time, it shows the founder strategically planned. Lastly, the time represents how quickly the founder and their team can deliver a product.

How many times have your customers re-ordered your product?

The reorder frequency doesn't always mean a customer for life. Though it's part of it, an investor wants to know if your customers are coming back to purchase from you. Do they want or need your product? If you sell soaps and most customers only purchase from you once, a red flag goes up. This is an indicator of underlying problems with your product. Your pricing could be too high and considered a luxury item. The customer may feel your product is inferior to your competitors and switched. Considering the soap example, your soap may be too harsh for their skin, causing the customer to find a product more amenable to their body. If you're selling products with a short life cycle, you, as a founder, must ask why you don't have customers coming back.

If you sell cars and investors would expect a customer to purchase once or twice. High-ticket items are often only purchased once or a few times over the customer's life. We do not limit one-time purchases to high dollar products. Consider products such as cast iron pans, storage containers, luggage, umbrellas, or backpacks. Though some are inexpensive, most consumers do not buy them regularly unless they're resellers.

Talk about the first step to complete your design.

Developing a product prototype is important. It provides investors and consumers with something they can see and feel. Prototypes don't start with the product. It starts with planning out the design. Understanding how you developed your product tells the investor how thorough you were in creating it.

What is your cost of goods (CoGs)?

Cost of goods sold represent a period (usually a year) where inventory to make a product is bought and sold.

Example: Let's take the example of John's COGs from last year. John's business held $50,000 worth of inventory to build their product in January. Luckily, he didn't need to purchase extra inventory and ended up with $20,000 worth of materials at the end of December.

COGS = Beginning Inventory + Inventory Purchases During the Period – Ending Inventory. With John's business, the COGs totaled $50,000 + $0 – $20,000 equals $30,000.

How much does it cost to make your product?

The cost to make the goods is a simple question, maybe not a simple answer. What is the cost of materials and labor? Add those two numbers together and you have developed your product cost. If you're the only person making the product and you're not paying yourself, mention the cost of materials and then mention the cost and labor if you hire someone to build the product. This provides a comprehensive understanding of the cost to scale.

What are your packaging costs?

An investor told me packaging only made a difference with products you can pick up and hold. Packaging anything greater than a vacuum cleaner didn't hold much importance. Packaging however is important to most products. It not only shows off the brand but creates a feeling as part of the customer experience.

Example: Over two hundred thousand Apple Evangelists have created video unboxing of their Apple products. It's part of the experience Apple creates for new and existing users. When I received my first iPhone, the unboxing of the phone became such an experience, I kept the box for years after I had no longer used the phone. With great packaging, comes a cost. Investors want to know if the cost of your packaging is worth it and how they might reduce cost and increase margins.

Who designed your packaging?

Many times, founders first create their own packaging. Early stage startups may use inexpensive options to outsource the initial design like Fiverr or using a friend from school who majored in graphic design. No matter who helped you create it, there's still thought going into the packaging and the designer needs to display it.

What is the cost to ship it?

All cost questions are areas an investor considers bringing cost down. Investors know shipping to be costly for most startups with a low volume of orders. Investors are more inquisitive on large products. Shipping could eat away at your margins, causing concern for the investor.

Who designed your product?

At the MVP stage, the investor hopes the founder did the initial design. You may lay it out on a napkin, but the founder must design the original idea. Though there may be some guidance from product developers, investors still want you to possess the vision for designing a great product.

Are you a product or a business?

This sounds like a trick question, however it's common to hear this question for new businesses. A product is a physical item you sell to a consumer. A business sells a product using people, processes, tools, and technology. The structure of a business enables a scalable product base to reach the hands of the customer who purchases it.

Why would stores carry your product?

Why stores must carry your product starts with your value proposition. What makes your company unique? Stores also consider the company's story. Why they entered this business and what is their vision. The stores want to know what's in it for them. What do the margins look like and how much revenue will they receive from one sale? This is the actual answer an investor is looking for. The amount you sell your product to consumers is higher than what you would sell it to a store for resale.

How and where do you sell your products?

Is your product sold in stores, through wholesalers, or online only? All suitable answers depending on your model and what works for your business. Using every source possible to sell your product makes little sense. Selling your product in stores is costly if your business is gaining extreme momentum online. Many online businesses have mastered selling strictly through their site and don't need other avenues of distribution.

Do you sell online?

Online sales have become popular, but not always the first method a founder chooses. You often hear founders start with selling to friends and family or at farmers' markets. Though many people think of technology when thinking of startup founders, not all founders are into technology or tech savvy.

Could you license your product?

The answer is typically "Yes, I could license my product." Follow up with your stance on licensing. Do you believe there would be a demand for licensing? The advantage is this is a low risk, high reward option to selling your product. The disadvantage is you lose control of how to distribute and package your product. If you possess an great story behind your product branding, it will probably be irrelevant once you license your product out. Also, working with a trustworthy licensee is important. They may have poor quality, not produce your product at all, or mislead you about the revenue they're generating in effect, leaving little or no money for you.

Is there a learning curve to using your product?

If there's a learning curve, your company must provide ways to bring the consumer to a place where they're up and running with your product quickly. It's important to have a strategy to lessen the learning curve and make your customer happy.

Where is your product produced?

Brands produce their product anywhere from their home kitchen to an overseas manufacturer. If you are not producing the product yourself, understand how and where it's produced. Just because your manufacturer is in Germany doesn't mean they produce your entire product there.

What is your production lead time?

In a digital age, the time between a customer clicking the "pay now" button to the time your product shows up on their doorstep is important. Investors understand this and want to make sure you're fulfilling the expectations of the customer in this way. A lot of products have a lead time of ten days or fewer unless it's a custom-made item. The expectation has shifted thanks to companies like Amazon. Customers now purchase products with same-day or next-day delivery along with free shipping.

How much inventory do you have?

Based on lean startup principles, have just enough inventory to fulfill your customers need when they want them. If you sell a hundred products a month, there's no reason you should have an inventory of one thousand products. As a startup, inventory is difficult to determine. Your product could go viral and within days your product inventory could hold zero items.

Do you have enough money to build up the inventory and put it into retail?

Most investors understand how expensive it can be to put your product into the retail market. There are numerous logistics involved and cost for premium shelf space. If you're raising money to grow into retail, it's important to complete the proper research to account for the expenses. Also, retail means you're charging wholesale prices which hold lesser margins for you than if you were to sell to an individual. Take this into account too.

How do you handle your logistics?

You'll hear logistics, fulfillment, and supply chain used synonymously. It is an important part of your business. This is part of what makes you a business and not a product. How you distribute your product to the customer adds to their customer satisfaction. As I always say, "Every product provides a service but not all services provide a product." Logistics is part of the service, and consistency is the name of the game.

Where does your product sit on store shelves?

Store placement is important. If you've ever gone into a grocery store and saw a product out of place, it's because of poor store placement. This is not any fault of the grocery; it's based on what the business pays for store placement. The founder pays more for better product placement. Once they become a well-known brand, placement does not matter as much.

Think of the candy aisle of your local grocery store. The candies with bright, fun colors are at the eye level of children, while the mints and chocolates are at the eye level of their parents. Same goes for the ice cream aisle. It's a strategy to persuade the target consumer to purchase the product within their natural line of sight.

How much do you have to pay for premium shelf space?

Research, research, research. Every store you want to distribute to will have a different rate based on the products they already sell. If you do not understand what they consider premium shelf space for your product, the retail company's rate sheet will show it. If you're in a retail store, you can observe the traffic of competing products to obtain a better understanding of the best locations.

Example: Some entrepreneurs have been daring enough to walk in stores they do business with and sell their own product. Sara Blakely, the founder of Spanx, is a well-known example of a bold founder. She told the Daily Mail, "I had no money to advertise, so I went out on the road and stood in department stores for nine hours a day, lifting my trouser leg to show customers my tights, and holding up pictures of my bottom, in my white trousers, with and without my product on." Investors want founders willing to be daring and scrappy like this.

Is your product well received by retailers?

If you're interested in retail, it's important to pitch your product to retailers like you pitch to investors. Retailers go through their own process of due diligence, vet your product against other products in their store and explain the selling possibilities.

Do you have samples I can see or try?

Investors want to touch and view your product. If you claim to own a product, investors want to receive a demonstration of how it works. If you possess a prototype, they want to hold it in their hands to get a feel of how a consumer will perceive it.

How does this product make it better, cheaper, and/or faster for your customer?

Alternate Question: How does your product add value?

This is your competitive advantage. This answers the question, "why should I buy yours versus your competitors' product?" Think about how it is better, cheaper, and/or faster than everyone else's product.

Can you mass produce your products and keep the same quality?

Some products are simple to make, others are more complex. If you're creating your product from your home or through a manufacturing partner, quality could be a concern. Investors want to know you're able to handle massive scale and you have quality controls in place.

Service Specific

How does your service make things better, cheaper, and/or faster for your customer?

Alternate question: How does your service add value?
This is your competitive advantage. This answers the question, "why should I buy yours versus your competitors' service?" Ideally, a customer wants to know they can get a service that's better and delivers faster results at a lower price. Base on importance, they may settle for one or two of the three.

How many return customers do you have?

It's important to understand actual numbers when you're in front of an investor. An idea may sound great, your business model may show great need and value, but if you are offering your service to the market and no one is buying again, there's a problem. Service businesses are more difficult to sell because you're usually selling a feeling or need before someone has the chance to experience it. With products, a potential customer can sample the product by touch, taste, or feel. They can also return products most of the time if they dislike it. Service businesses are different. They may not sample (outside of a trial version mostly done by SaaS companies).

Who performs the work for this service?

As companies expand, it's not uncommon for startups to outsource services to another startup or small business. This allows the company to scale and create partnerships. NOTE: If this is the case, an investor wants to view the structure of the partnership agreement.

What is your customer retention rate?

The key number is 25%. It sounds low, but most startups early adopters of the service will show brand loyalty based on the features you continue to roll out or the expanded capabilities of your services. That's the sweet spot guaranteeing the business will probably stay afloat.

Companies use the Net Promoter Score (NPS) as a metric to gauge customer loyalty for the brand and services provided. Apple has been using NPS as part of their employee recognition and customer engagement for years.

Creating an NPS survey is easy. There are tons of examples and templates on the internet. Go to www.afterthepitch.com/resources to download your own. Companies ask customers to rate their service on a 0 to 10 scale. They break the customers down into Promoters, Passives, and Detractors.

Promoters are your biggest advocates. They're likely your early adopters who took a chance on your company and loved it from the start.

Passives believe your services are average but are more likely to become Promoters as your service model matures. These are the people you need to engage with the most. They will provide much feedback because they feel they are part of growing your service business.

Detractors are customers who dislike your service. It may be their first time using it, they may have had a poor experience with an employee, or they only go to you because they need what you offer and there are no other options. Based on the rating, you can tell the type of customer service each person received along with what category they fall under. Use this with your retention rate to find issues in your service.

Run through the process of how your service works?

Having a formal process to the service you provide adds consistency, ways to measure performance, and puts an investor at ease knowing you're not flying by the seat of your pants when performing a service.

How do you ensure the quality of your service stays consistent as you scale?

After you've shown the process to the investor, make sure they know you have guardrails in place to measure the company's efficiency. Not all service businesses provide a one-size fits all model.

How do you regulate change?

When your business changes, how do you moderate the change? Change comes both internally and externally to your business. Managing change must be part of your startup strategy. Internally, your processes may change as you bring in more employees. One process may also change another. Externally, economic changes can have a major effect on how your business runs. How do you manage this change?

Chapter Fourteen: Industry-Specific

Technology

Tech investing is what I love, and it has become the lifeblood of investing. Mostly when you think about Venture Capital and seed stage funding, the first organization coming to mind is a company like Facebook, Google, Uber, or PayPal.

Is your business really a business or is it a feature?

In technology, investors concern themselves with how easily technology is replicated. If the technology is so niche a larger company could quickly duplicate it with their massive development team and deploy it to their large list of users, this may be a feature and not a business. A founder must portray why their technology is an actual scalable business instead of just a feature.

How are you disrupting your industry?

This partially goes back to the minimal viable product (MVP). What value is your technology providing? What parts of it is going to change the way customers work or live? Uber and Lyft changed the way people get around. Airbnb changed the way travelers booked their stay.

Where do you see the technology going in the next 2-3 years?

Previously the book stated a similar question as it related to the industry. As a founder, having a vision for how the technology can scale with the foreseeable industry changes will put the founder ahead of most. The strategies and business models often seen however do not consider disruptors coming into the industry or major industry changes.

Is this a fad?

This has become more and more of a discussion for investors as the app market has become saturated and VR has yet taken a major foothold in the technology space. Investors view tons of businesses and it's often easy to understand a business is going to become a fad right away.

What do you see as the next generation or version of your software/hardware?

This is where a company's product roadmap is extremely important. The company can already be thinking several versions ahead of where they are in the development process. With funding or not, a product roadmap answers this question.

Who does the manufacturing of your hardware?

These sound like pretty basic questions, but the quality and reputation of the company who makes your hardware is very important. Your partnerships are very important to an investor because it can make or break your profits. Manufacturers determine your time to customer, influence your fulfillment quality, warehousing, and overall product quality.

Who does the development of your software?

Same as for manufacturing, an investor wants to grasp the quality and reputation of your software. Software companies or individual developers can determine how updates and security settings are set. The experience of the person or company can also tell an investor how quickly the company delivers. It also determines the quality of the delivered product.

Questions an Investor Should Not Ask

Can I view your code?

I've heard of investment teams stealing a founder's code before. Though the code may be proprietary, a corporation who has the financial backing to take the code and quickly launch a product or company may have a good argument to being the owners of the code. All they have to do is prove to a court their code is slightly different.

Also, there are employees who will leave a startup to form another. Companies such as Avant, Inc. and Bumble had founders or employees leave the company to start their own. In both cases, the lawsuits over code or feature ownership caused disorder for all parties.

How is your code built?

It's fine for investors to ask about the coding language or the type of database used to store data, but be light on details which aids someone in copying your software.

What is your proprietary algorithm?

Examples: Dating apps *Tinder* and *Bumble* have been in a court battle to determine who owns the "swipe left" feature. *Tinder* created the swipe left features however when employee, Whitney Wolfe Herd, left the company and sued over sexual harassment claims, she created *Bumble*. The dating app *Tinder* has tried several times to buy *Bumble*. After no success, they decided to sue *Bumble* for stealing proprietary information. *Bumble* just believed the lawsuit was to negate the already active sexual harassment suit.

This incident happens a lot however some not publicized. It has sparked questions on what is proprietary and patentable in the software world. When owning an innovative company, detailed data and information must be secured with only those who need to know. This shouldn't stop you from telling people about your business, but you must know what areas of your business you must secure.

Health

Has your product been tested and approved by the FDA?

For health products, founders must abide by all the regulations required to be checked off before selling to a customer. Giving false claims not only creates reputational risk but it also deters investors from wanting to provide you funding. Even more important, it could put customers in danger.

Will this solution dramatically improve customers' lives?

Once again, false claims are prohibited. An investor wants to know if your product will work and is it scientifically proven to work.

How have you dealt with regulation restrictions?

A founder or one of their team members must be on top of regulation and it must be their number one priority to become a legally sound company. By following the health regulations, you lessen the risk of lawsuits.

What are the barriers to entry in the market?

Obviously for health products, laws, rules, and regulations are a barrier to entry, but often there are more reasons making it difficult to gain a footprint into the market.

Can this be integrated with a person's insurance?

Integration with other health care plans or systems is important. The lack of integrations is more prevalent than the features a system has.

Example: Cerner and Epic are two software titans in the healthcare industry. They build electronic health record (EHR) systems which houses their customers' patient records. These competitors have customers all over the country and have caused hospitals (their main customer segment) heartache when working to figure out which company to work with. The problem is these two systems do not integrate with one another. If a patient goes to a hospital who uses a Cerner system, then years later goes to another healthcare company who uses Epic's system, they cannot easily transfer the patient record to one another.

Will it be over the counter or a prescribed product?

There's a line between over the counter (OTC) and prescribed drugs, creams, and ointments. Typically, OTC fits in a basic criterion; They can be self-administered for a self-diagnosis with a low risk the user will abuse the drug. There are more criteria, but this sums it up for a founder with a general idea of what their product is. As you develop the product, clinical research companies will determine what your product options are.

Have you completed clinical trials or where are you in the trial stage?

After numerous studies and initial testing, drugs must go through a four-stage clinical trial. At each stage, different tests must be passed on a potential user (whether it be a human or animal). As you go through the stages, more users must participate in the trial to determine validity. They use these phases to evaluate consumption, safety, side-effects, and effectiveness for the person or animal.

Have you considered other countries where regulation is not as stringent?

In the United States, the Food and Drug Administration (FDA) approves what drugs can be sold in the US. Though some drugs are restricted by the FDA, they're sold outside of the country. Drug makers find other countries who have low barriers to entry and market their products there instead. Drug prices are also higher in the US. Some consumers find it less expensive to purchase the products they need outside of the states. This causes companies to find other countries possessing less stringent regulations and where they can make a greater profit.

Financial Services

How do you keep up with the ever-evolving regulatory landscape?

Founders are in the financial or financial technology (fintech) space must keep up with the laws and regulations. There're many ways to do it, but how will you as a founder keep up with these changes?

How do you make sure the financial data you share is standardized, accurate, and secure?

Financial data (and all other types of data) must be standardized, accurate, and secure. Financial data not having these attributes are liable to have increased risk and more liability for the company and investor. What kind of infrastructure and standards do you have in place to make sure these three attributes exist in your company? Your company may also receive data from other sources. As a financial founder, it's important to know what your company is doing to make sure your data is standardized, accurate, and secure. Whatever you share with the customer must be right or they will not trust your brand and you will lose them.

What is your routine for customer follow-up?

Processes are important to any company. Customer follow-up is part of creating an outstanding impression on your clients and can also create opportunities for referrals and the customer to buy from you again.

Does your business have the correct permits, licenses, and certifications to operate legally?

We have not come across a financial services company not needing at least a license or certification. Founders must have done their research to verify what they need. Not having the right credentials could lead to major lawsuits and unhappy investors.

Did you start your business because you are passionate about your idea or because you want to cash in on the latest trend?

Technology and financial services startups are often created because of trends or gaps in the market. A founder possessing a financial background provides additional credibility to your startup. An excellent story of why you developed your company can entice an investor to inject capital into your startup. Starting a business without having a passion for it can hinder long term growth.

What niche are you covering?

Many financial services companies start off with a niche they target, then expand to other areas within the financial services ring. The niche could be related to product or customer. If one of the company's products are high performing or beats out the competitors, it is considered the company's niche.

A friend in my entrepreneurs group runs a fintech (financial technology) company who serves individuals who feel they do not have enough money to invest. The company aims to help build wealth for all people, regardless of financial status. His business is revolutionary not only because you can invest such a small amount but included are planning tools and advice from Certified Financial Planners™. That's a feature rarely afforded to all socioeconomic levels.

Can you provide the essentials to certifying this is the right niche to be in?

The financial services businesses are sometimes so difficult to enter in because of the behemoths like New York Life, Bank of

America, and JP Morgan. The founder must take a second look at their strategy in the financial services industry and it's okay to pivot. To do this, founders must review and/or fine tune these four documents:

- Market Assessments
- Competitive Analysis
- Marketing Plan
- Sales Plan

Hospitality (including Food and Beverage)

Who owns the customer?

Hospitality is one of the industries in which your customers may come to you through other means.

Example: As a hotel owner, your customers could come mainly from *Travelocity*. This means *Travelocity* owns the customer. Your customer acquisition process however could turn the *Travelocity* customer into your customer. Until the hotel has direct access to a customer, they do not own the customer.

What do you do to combat your competition?

The hospitality market is saturated with companies who do the "same thing". In my history and research of the hospitality industry there are few disruptors in the industry. Most companies who want to break into this market and make extreme changes are looking for ways to keep costs low and occupancy high. For a technology company to come in and disrupt, they must obtain some real value, especially in sectors like hotels and motels where technology is not a priority to profits.

What kind of analytics do you have to prove success and make customer actions predictable?

The hospitality industry has many great opportunities to collect data about their customer. The hospitality industry can gather:

- Sales on products and services
- The time products and services sell the best
- The location receiving the most sells
- The most salespeople making the most sells
- Trends in purchasing
- Demographic of who is purchasing
- Feedback on how the customer felt about the products and services

Other companies can also receive this information; however, hospitality is a high touch industry. Companies are selling both an experience and a feeling which determines the customers' likelihood of buying repeatedly and referring more people. As a founder, understand the important data and continuously make decisions based on the data. It's best to start tracking it with the first customer.

Where do you source your food/beverage ingredients?

In the food or beverage industry, sourcing ingredients influences three major areas; quality, cost, and logistics. Ingredients can be part of the company's story. Artisans pride themselves on locally source ingredients. "Farm-to-table" menu items are trending more in metro-based restaurants as documentaries are informing consumers of the health disadvantages of big box suppliers. Beverage companies also pride themselves on natural ingredients. The question here is not only where do you source your ingredients, but why do you source your ingredients there? If it's for an insignificant reason, think quality, cost, and convenience/logistics.

Pitch Dictionary

accelerator: a program to help startup founders speed up their growth by creating a small community of founders and providing them with the right people and resources(such as mentorship, sales, marketing, product design, research, etc.) to grow and scale their companies.

angel: an investor who individually provides capital to startups in exchange for convertible debt or equity stake(ownership) in the business.

accounts receivable (A/R): money owed to a company by its debtors.

attrition rate: the number of customers or employees you lose per year over the customers that you have. This number is show in a percentage. Example: If you have 1000 customers and you lose 200 this year, you will calculate 200/1000 = 0.2 which gives you an attrition rate of 20%.

bootstrap: solely using the profit from your startup to fund its growth.

bottom line: the company's net income.

bridge note: a short-term loan used to float a company between a pivot, major company change, or the next funding round is secured.

burn rate: the rate in which a business can operate before it runs out of money.

business model: a framework that explains the who, what, how, and why of a company which gives it the legs to become a successful company. Some Founders build out the business model before diving into the business plan.

business plan: a detailed document displaying a company's goals, projected financials, and other future strategies and objectives.

buyout: the act of purchasing all ownership shares in a business.

cap (valuation cap): the maximum price that your convertible note will convert into equity. It will incentivize the investor to put their money in early and lock them in at a discount rate before the business's valuation grows.

cap (capitalization) table: a chart that lays out the ownership of all investors and what they invested to receive their ownership.

capped convertible note: an investment originally taken as a loan that has the option of converting into equity stake at a maximum valuation.

cash flow: the amount of cash flowing in and out of a business.

churn rate: for business with a subscription model, this is the percentage that people cancel or do not renew their subscription.

close the round: a point in which a founder stops taking new investment funding for their startup.

cost of goods sold (COGS): the price for a founder/startup to produce a product or service including materials and labor.

competitive advantage: features and attributes of a business, product, or services that makes customers want to buy from that business versus its competitor(s).

common stock (also known as voting shares or ordinary shared): equity ownership in a company allowing the equity owner to vote on the election of board of directors and corporate policy

contingency: a funding commitment made based on future results.

conversion rate: a metric that varies by company and product or service but leads to the percentage that a lead or customer is converted into a customer of a (another) product or service.

convertible note (or convertible debt): a initial loan given by an investor. During the next round of investing, a third-party may then set the value of the startup business. The initial investor then has the option of converting that loan value into equity stake in the startup.

crowdfunding: a way to raise money through large groups of people (usually over the internet) in exchange for a product or service once the product or service has been launched.

customer acquisition cost (CAC - /kak/): the sales and marketing cost related to turning a person into a customer.

customer discovery: a stage in product/service development where a company learns from the voice of the customer (VOC) how they can best produce or optimize their product/service. Customer discovery is usually conducted through phone calls, surveys, or focus groups.

Also see: Voice of the Customer (VOC)

deal flow: the process and rate in which an investment firm can intake new startups and provide them capital.

design patents: patents that cover the design or appearance of an invention. Usually valid for 14 years.

dilution: a decrease in founder, investor, and/or shareholder ownership/equity when a new investor provides funding or new shares are distributed.

direct to consumer (D2C or DTC): a sells method where a brand provides their product to the end user/customer versus using a third-party retailer or distributor.

earnings before interest, taxes, depreciation, and amortization (EBITDA): a measurement used by companies to track financial performance.

equity (also known as equity stake, equity ownership, or equity percentage): the amount of ownership (usually in the form of a percentage) a person owns of a company.

family office: a privately owned wealth management group of wealth family members who invest in a variety of assets.

fintech: short for financial technology.

friends and family round: the initial stage of funding in which a founders asks people they know to invest into their company.

Also see: pre-seed funding

funding: money provided for the growth of a business.

fund: a pool of money from multiple investors used for investment of one or more companies.

gross income: gross revenue minus cost of goods sold

incubator: a program to help startup founders create innovative products (usually technology related) by creating a small community of founders and providing them with the right people and resources (such as mentorship, sales, marketing, product design, research, etc.) to create their business model and companies.

initial coin offering (ICO): a stage in a company's growth in which they raise funds using cryptocurrency.

initial public offering (IPO): a stage in a company's growth in which they launch themselves as a company on the stock market.

landed cost: the total price of a product or shipment once it has arrived at a buyer's doorstep. The landed cost can include the original price of the product, transportation fees (both inland and ocean), customs, duties, taxes, tariffs, insurance, currency conversion, crating, handling and payment fees.

letter of intent (LOI): a statement provided to a business by a customer show they they intend to be a customer in the near future depend certain stipulations such as fulfillment capabilities, logistics, and cost reduction.

lifetime value (LTV) (average lifetime value): the revenue a customer brings in through the period in which they are a customer. Example: If a company's average customer used their $50/month subscription services for 5 years and that brought in revenue of $3,000, their lifetime value would be $3,000.

line of business: a division in a busines or industry focusing on a single product or group of similar products.

margins (profit margins): the net income divided by net sales.

market capitalization (market cap): the total value of all shares of stock a company possesses.

material customer: a consumer (usually a company) who consumes the largest amount (in revenue) of your products or services. They can either use, distribute, or sell your product to other consumers. Either way, it generates a large amount of revenue for the startup.

mergers and acquisitions (M&A): the event which a company buys another and the two companies combine into one.

micro loans: A small loan provided by an individual or group of individuals that is not issued by a credit union or bank.

minimum viable product (MVP): a product, service, or idea with just enough features to sell to a customer or test market feasibility.

most favored nation (MFN): a country providing the most advantageous investment terms by another country.

net income: business sales minus cost of goods sold, general expenses, interest, and taxes.

net sales: the sum of a company's gross sales minus its discounts, allowances, and returns.

oversubscribe: when a founder has raised more money than what is needed or asked for during a particular funding round.

patent pending: a stage of the patent process where the patent has been filed. This puts the patent under temporary protection in case someone tries to "knock off" the product or file a patent for it. Investors have to keep in mind that only 52% of patents are actually approved.

per-share earnings (EPS): a company's net profits divided by the number of common shares it has outstanding.

perpetuity: a return strategy that investors use that consists of a payback of a percentage or dollar amount for an indefinite period of time.

pitch deck: a brief presentation usually used by a founder that gives an overview of the business, it's traction, and/or it's progress. This document is used to secure funding.

pre-seed funding: the earliest stage of raising capital when a company has developed a minimal viable product (MVP) and has started testing the viability of the product.

Also see: friends and family round

preferred stock: equity ownership in a company that does not allow the owner to vote on corporate policy or electing members of the board of directors

price-to-earnings (P/E) ratio: the company's current share price relative to its per-share earnings (EPS).

private equity: a later stage of funding where a company raises funds to purchase a startup, small, medium, or large company that has not reached IPO.

pro forma: a detailed document providing financial projections based on confident assumptions about the company and market.

proprietary: related to ownership of a process or trade secret of the company.

profit and loss (P&L): a financial document summarizing costs, expenses, and revenue acquired over a exact period of time.

profit margin: Profit Margin = (Net Profit / Revenue) * 100%

raise: a short way of saying fundraise; an amount of money to be secured for startup investment.

real estate investment trust (REIT): a funding vehicle owned by a publicly traded company who uses other people's capital to fund real estate projects.

return on investment (R.O.I.): the ratio of net profit vs net cost that determines if a company or product is a smart financing decision. High R.O.I. means you made a smart decision while low R.O.I. means you did not make a intelligent decision or need to review ways to optimize profits and/or reduce cost.

round: the separate periods of funding that a startup goes through to valuate/re-valuate their company and raise more capital.

Also See: seed funding

Also See: pre-seed funding

Also See: friends and family round

Also See: series A, series B, series C

royalty: a type of payback to investors that includes either a certain dollar amount or percentage that should be given back to the investor based on sales or net profit.

run rate: run rate is the forecast of sales or revenue based on a current period of financial data.

runway: the amount of money the business has on hand divided by its run rate – it tells you how long the business can continue its current trajectory without emptying the bank account.

software as a service (SaaS): a business model where software is built using cloud computing and a third-party provider hosts the software for customers to use.

seed funding (or seed capital): financing offered to the founder(s) of a company to help started their business.

security: a tradable financial asset such as a stock or bond.

series A: a company's first round of investment by Venture Capitalists and the second round of investment for startup funding.

series B: a company's second round of investment by Venture Capitalists and the third round of investment for startup funding.

series C: a company's third round of investment by Venture Capitalists and the fourth round of investment for startup funding.

shares: a representation of equity ownership of company that is broken down into units versus equity percentage.

stock options: for the protection of an investor, this gives an investor the ability to buy or sell a stock at an agreed upon amount and time.

SWOT analysis: a technique for evaluating the strengths, weaknesses, opportunities, and threats of a company.

syndicate: a group of investors pooling money together to fund a business.

top line: a company's gross sales or revenues.

term sheet: a high-level document outlining the business agreement between the founder and the investor.

uncapped convertible note: an investment originally taken as a loan that has the option of converting into equity stake at an unknown valuation.

unicorn: a business with +$1 billion valuation. Less than 0.07% of venture-backed companies maintain this status. There have been 39 unicorns since 2003 which it's about 4 companies every year.

upfit (or fitout): is the tenant improvement work within an empty commercial shell space. The landlord typically provides HVAC and electrical services stubbed into the space, along with the separation walls between tenants- the rest is up to the renter and becomes the "tenant fitout".

utility patents: patents that cover the functional parts of an invention. Patents typically valid for 20 years.

valuation: the dollar amount in which a founder, investor, or analyst/appraiser estimates that a company is worth.

value proposition (or value prop): a specific and sometimes unique benefit that a company delivers to it's customers through its product or service.

venture capitalist (VC): a person or firm who invests time and/or money into company with the expectations of a high growth return.

voice of the customer (VOC): the process of finding out what a customer wants by asking the customer directly.

References

1. https://corp.delaware.gov/aboutagency/
2. https://www.brex.com/blog/burn-rates/
3. https://www.reit.com/data-research/research/nareit-research/87-million-americans-own-reit-stocks
4. https://www.sec.gov/files/2017-03/RegCF_WhitePaper.pdf
5. https://paulcollege.unh.edu/sites/default/files/resource/files/2018-analysis-report.pdf

Adrian T. Marable is an entrepreneur and the author of After the Pitch, a new investor and founder's guide to early-stage startup investing. What Adrian does best is take an aerial view of his coaching clients' problems and help them build a roadmap to success. As an angel investor he coaches and mentors entrepreneurs and college students, helping them articulate their business, build operational strategies and determine the right business models.

His ability to be both technical and business savvy has allowed him to bridge a major gap between technical and non-technical founders. Among his nine certifications around business operations and process improvement, Adrian holds a Bachelor of Science degree in Electrical Engineering from Old Dominion University and a Master of Business Administration with a concentration in Finance from Queens University of Charlotte. Prior to writing this book, Adrian began his career in the financial services industry and later moved into the field of engineering and IT.

In 2009, Adrian founded an IT company, Groopwork, that works with small businesses to expand their digital reach through website design, application development and IT support. Groopwork's training division provides a flagship Learning Management System (LMS), GroopED, and he has over a dozen trainers who provide corporate training to help business teams work more effectively and become agile in their industries.

With over 20 years of experience in technology, Adrian has worked with some of the biggest organizations in the world to help them with corporate transformations, mergers, acquisitions, and divestitures including the Department of Defense, Manufacturing Techniques, Inc., Ingersoll Rand, and Bank of America.

Adrian resides in North Carolina with his wife (Ebony) and daughter (Payton).

www.ingramcontent.com/pod-product-compliance
Lightning Source LLC
Chambersburg PA
CBHW071811080526
44589CB00012B/750